ADVANCE PRAISE FOR *SCORE!*

"I often judge a book by the number of journal pages my notes fill by the time I turn the last page. *Score!* passes this test with flying colors. *Score!* made me take a hard look at where I am as a data-driven manager and gave me concrete steps on ways to improve: I felt energized and ready to mine for data the very next day. If you want to better utilize data in your fundraising work—read *Score!* today."

Jennifer Roccanti • Director of Development • Miriam's Kitchen

"*Score!* helps the advancement professional realize that data is our friend. Data-driven decision making produces tangible return on investment. Everyone in the higher education and nonprofit sector should read it!"

Robb Drury • Associate Vice President, Advancement Operations • San Jose State University

"Wylie and his team helped me reinvent the annual fund at San Francisco State University. While I had worked with data-driven campaigns for years in the private sector, the higher ed space seemed oblivious to the use of data mining and statistics to raise money from their extensive databases. Within 18 months, management at SF State were fully on-board with using Wylie's methodology and still use it today. This book will show you how to up your fundraising game using the knowledge you already have about your donors."

George Machun • Director of Communications & Marketing
California State University, Monterey Bay

"This book is the cure for too many strategic meetings that include the words 'I think' or 'I feel' in regard to whom we should be targeting for our marketing. Data-driven decisions are the way to go, and MacDonell and Wylie prove it is not impossible for any organization—regardless of how big your database or how many staff you employ."

Pamela D. Leonard • National Operations, Charitable Estate Planning
American Heart Association

"*Score!* certainly is not a typical read on statistical analysis. The personal touch brought by MacDonell and Wylie makes this book totally enjoyable to read. I recommend it to all vice presidents and other powers-that-be in the fundraising arena. The results speak for themselves. With the use of predictive models supplied by Peter Wylie and John Sammis, we far surpassed our comprehensive campaign goal."

Joan M. Sullivan • Assistant Director of Prospect Research • Connecticut College

"Using humor and real-life examples, MacDonell and Wylie make the case, and provide the blueprint, for utilizing analytics in advancement. This how-to guide explains how advancement offices in nonprofit institutions of all sizes can reap the benefits of analytics. Analytics in development is all about better (best?) use of the reams of data we all have on hand, with limited time and resources. Wylie and MacDonell explain how to take the data out of its comfort zone, the 'homey confines of your database,' and put it to work. Confirm or deny long-held assumptions or hunches about your constituents. Help development officers identify your best major, annual fund, and planned giving prospects. Make some 'mental sausage.' The possibilities are virtually endless and the results will pay for themselves many times over."

Frank Loucka • Director of Advancement S
Denison Uni

"MacDonell and Wylie have authored an outstanding work that is filled with great stories and, most important, an airtight argument for data-driven decision making. *Score!* is a pleasure to read and an absolute must for anyone who works in nonprofit fundraising."

James Vineburgh • Director of Research • TWG Plus

"If your organization is slow to becoming a data-driven organization or intimidated by analytics, read this now. MacDonell and Wylie provide excellent instruction, case studies, and stories for how to jump on board."

Corbett Shinn • Reporting and Analytics Manager • Haverford College

"In *Score!*, MacDonell and Wylie cover all the bases of analytics—what it's all about, how to get there, and what it can do for you and your organization. There is no better resource than this book to 'make the case' for the effective implementation of data-driven analytics, with thoughtful discussion on tangential benefits. By offering practical, comprehensive, and substantiated applications, the authors foster intense enthusiasm in data geeks and non–data geeks alike with this quick-read gem—a true 'guiding light' for any well-developed advancement program."

Lisette Clem • Director of Advancement Services • Bryant University

"The best thing advancement departments can do to raise more money isn't necessarily hiring more staff—it's using the information they already have to identify their most likely donors. *Score!* makes the case for thoughtful, thorough data-driven analysis in an approachable way. Everyone, including gift officers, vice presidents, and alumni directors, will see how looking at your data in new and innovative ways will pay off over and over again."

Donna Ancypa Holmes • Annual Fund Director and Fundraising Consultant

"*Score!* takes a dry topic and makes it entertaining. MacDonell and Wylie have a keen understanding of the data issues that most nonprofits face, and I can say from experience that data modeling works. After Wylie created a custom model for our organization, we had a *significant* improvement in our acquisition campaign. I strongly recommend this book to any fundraising professional who is tired of stagnant results and wants to find the gold nuggets hidden in their database."

Todd Prepsky • Annual Giving Consultant

"Rarely have I come across such a persuasive plan for how we can reach our highest potential from two who understand the business so profoundly. They addresses our everyday problems; ones that have become so much a part of our lives that we hardly see them. *Score!* delivers solutions from two who know the fundraising business, warts and all, and understand the full potential, appallingly unrealized though it may be."

Rita Dibble • Director of Alumni Relations and Annual Giving
Lincoln University in Pennsylvania

"Analytics and predictive modeling are more than a trend in advancement—they are an approach and discipline integral to strategic and tactical decision-making and prospect identification. *Score!* is eminently practical, with concrete examples and realistic advice for typical challenges and true-to-life situations."

Christina Pulawski • Research Prospect Management • Information Flow for Fund Raising

sc*ore!

sc*ore!

Data-Driven Success for
Your Advancement Team

KEVIN MacDONELL & PETER B. WYLIE

Washington, D.C.

Library of Congress Cataloging-in-Publication Data

MacDonell, Kevin.
 Score! : data-driven decision-making for the entire advancement team / Kevin MacDonell and Peter Wylie.
  pages cm.
 Includes bibliographical references and index.
 ISBN 978-0-89964-445-5 (pbk. : alk. paper) 1. Educational fund raising—Data processing. 2. Universities and colleges—Alumni and alumnae. I. Title.

LB2335.95.M33 2014
379.1'3—dc23

2014000398

Designer: Judy Myers, Graphic Design
Art Director: Angela Carpenter Gildner
Editorial Directors: Julie K. Schorfheide and Doug Goldenberg-Hart

COUNCIL FOR ADVANCEMENT
AND SUPPORT OF EDUCATION®

CASE
1307 New York Avenue, NW
Suite 1000
Washington, DC 20005-4701

CASE Europe
3rd Floor, Paxton House
30 Artillery Lane
London E1 7LS
United Kingdom

CASE Asia-Pacific
Unit 05-03
Shaw Foundation
Alumni House
11 Kent Ridge Drive
Singapore 119244

CASE América Latina
Berlín 18 4to piso, Colonia Juárez
Código Postal 06600, México D.F.
Delegación Cuauhtémoc
México

Contents

Acknowledgments

Kevin MacDonell

My portions of this book were written mainly at home, mostly during early mornings before heading to work. I owe thanks to my wife, **Leslie Smith**, for putting up with a closed door during these solitary hours. I must also thank **Peter Wylie**; before he was my co-writer, he was my data-mining instructor (with **John Sammis**), and later my mentor and friend. I am fortunate to continue learning from him long past the end of that training contract. What I have not learned from Peter, I learned on the job by playing with real data, and among my co-workers and employers I must thank: **Bernardine MacDonald**, coordinator of advancement records at St. Francis Xavier University in Antigonish, Nova Scotia, who answered my earliest naïve questions about data and who handed me my first copy of Peter Wylie's book *Data Mining for Fund Raisers;* **Iain Boyd**, retired director, advancement relations at St.F.X. University, who brought me into prospect research and made room for me to pursue my experiments with alumni data; **Floyd Dykeman**, vice president, external relations, at Dalhousie University, who understands the future belongs to institutions that learn to make use of the investment in their databases to best serve students, alumni, and donors; and **Peter Fardy**, chief development officer and assistant vice president, external relations, at Dalhousie, who probably more than anyone else has recognized my interest in data analysis as an opportunity for both of us, allowing me to turn what was once just an interesting sideline project into a career. And finally, I thank the readers of my blog, **CoolData.org**, with whom I've had the pleasure of carrying on a conversation since 2009.

Peter Wylie

Lest the band start playing like it does at the Oscar and Golden Globe award ceremonies, I shall strive for brevity here.

Kevin MacDonell. This book would not have been written without Kevin's gift for putting words together, his discipline, his passion for data analytics, and his willingness to put up with my curmudgeonness. He has and will continue to be a pleasure to work with and a great friend. One more thing. The opportunity to contribute to his terrific blog has helped keep my passion for data analytics burning brightly at an age when the flame might otherwise have started to flicker.

Linda Margolis Wylie. Linda is my spouse of almost 38 years and the best thing that has ever happened to me. She has always been a cheerleader for everything I have written over our decades together. Several years back I wrote a novel about my paternal grandfather who lived through a combat zone in South Carolina in the 1860s. I read every word of every draft aloud to her. By the end she knew the characters better than I did.

John Sammis. I can't say enough about this guy as both a friend and a colleague. He knows how much I appreciate him, and he knows I would never have made a second career out of my love for analytics without him.

Julie Schorfheide. Ah ... Julie. The consummate professional editor. A classy lady who is not in the least put off by my ribald sense of humor. She cut her teeth in the city room of a major southern newspaper where some of those good ole boy reporters would have made me look like a prude.

Clients and prospective clients. There have been hundreds of them over the last 15 years. As much as my graduate training and technical reading have taught me, these folks have taught me far more. Their data and their desire to understand it and help their missions with it have stretched my skills and my knowledge enormously.

You readers. Without you there would be no reason to set words down on paper. Your willingness to plow through things we write keeps us going. And when you tell us that you gained something from one of our articles or books, it makes all the effort and energy we've expended so very worthwhile. Thank you. Thank you very much.

Join the online discussion
If you're on Twitter, use the hashtag #scorethebook to find discussion related to this book, and contribute your own thoughts.

Introduction
Don't Skip This Introduction

Are you the type who plows into the meat of a book without reading the introduction? Yeah, so are we. But we ask that you read this one, because we've got a couple of important things to tell you, and we have some pointers about how you might use this book to change your organization. That's right—this is not just for your entertainment. You are going to use this book to change the way you and your institution go about business.

A tall order? Yes. But we will do what we can, and the rest will be up to you.

Later we'll tell you a little about us and why we put this book together. But for the moment, let's focus on who you are and why you might be spending your time and energy on what we've written. Rightly or wrongly, we assume you have the equivalent of one of these six job titles:

- Director of the annual fund,
- Director of prospect research,
- Director of major giving,
- Director of alumni relations,
- Data analyst (or someone who would like to have that title), or
- Vice president of advancement/development.

Here's our sense of some of the stresses and strains you endure week in and week out.

Director of the annual fund
This is a tough job. There's a lot of pressure on you to meet giving goals by two dates: the end of the tax year (December 31) and the end of the fiscal year (June 30 for many). You and the folks you work for are constantly looking at what gifts

have come in compared to this time last year and compared to goals you may not have had much say in setting.

Director of prospect research
You may not experience the same day-to-day pressure as your annual fund director colleague, but you have plenty of things to worry about. You're constantly on the hunt for people in your database who may be poised to make a major gift, especially when you're in the midst of a big campaign. You and the people who work for you find good candidates, and you put those candidates in front of gift officers. Then you stretch the limits of your patience and persuasiveness to get those gift officers to reach out to these prospects to get big money that would not otherwise come in.

Director of major giving
You're in charge of the "sales force" of folks who go out and deal with the heavy-hitting donors. Some of these folks are truly talented. You can cut them loose and let them go out and work their magic, even if they seem helter-skelter and as temperamental as your teenage son or daughter. Others of them never leave the office as they continue their quixotic quest for that yet-to-be-uncovered donor whose name will one day appear on a hall or a wing or some other impressive edifice. While you worry about their lack of productivity, you do the best you can with deans and board members and the president or CEO who are hell-bent on meeting that daunting campaign goal.

Director of alumni relations
Ah yes, the alumni. Such a varied lot, aren't they? Some of them are gems and have become good friends and make your job so much easier than it would be if they weren't there for you. A lot of them are … well, they're sort of like ghosts: They're pretty much invisible. And then there are a small few who are a monumental pain in the tuchis, even if they do great stuff for the institution. It's almost as if you're in charge of a party where some of the guests never go home and allow you to clean up the house so you can go to bed and get some sleep.

Data analyst (or someone who would like to have that title)
Hang on. We'll be spending a lot of time with you shortly.

Vice president of advancement/development
We know that you have huge pressures in your job, most of it coming from people who control your fate. The board. The president or CEO. Influential alumni and patrons. We empathize. But for the nonce, we'd like you to set aside that pressure

and read as much of this book as you can, your bursting-at-the-seams schedule notwithstanding. Just read. We'll check back in with you later.

Whoever you are, this book is about you, even though it seems to be mostly pre-occupied with the subject of "data."

Data is a major character in this book. At no time have businesses and non-profits had so much of their own data to work with, so much cheap computing power to analyze it with, and so many ways to train their current staff in analyti-cal methods. Awareness of the importance of data analysis is at an all-time high—the buzz at conferences is all about analytics, data mining, predictive modeling, and "big data." Even as the subject grows increasingly attractive for its own sake, some institutions are also being forced to adopt data-driven methods in order to deal with shrinking budgets, ever-growing constituencies, and increased scrutiny around the amount of money charities spend to raise a dollar.

You would think, then, that data-driven decision-making would be the rule rather than the exception. Unfortunately, organizations in the nonprofit sector have lagged far behind their counterparts in the world of business. During the process of writing this book, we have flip-flopped on the question of whether the future looks rosy or gloomy for nonprofit institutions. At times it seems that years of preaching about data has made almost no dent in the attitudes of higher educa-tion decision-makers—and yet, every year, more and more of the individual staff members who work for them are getting turned on to analyzing data, regardless of whether they have any previous experience. We have despaired that although upper-management types love to throw around fancy terms such as *analytics,* there is very little real work being done to justify the self-congratulation—and yet, given the increased availability of work skills and computing power, and a growing awareness of the value of data generally, progress seems inevitable.

So we may not have a handle on where the sector is really going, or how long it will take to get there. But we know this: There are some serious gaps to be bridged. In some institutions, the leadership is aware of the importance of data, but they don't know how to build the capacity to do something about it. In other institutions, keen individuals on staff are doing what they can to learn and apply new methods to their own work, but they lack support from their employers in trying to promote innovation across the organization. In either case, progress is limited by the fact that a data-oriented mindset does not permeate the organiza-tion from top to bottom.

This book is our attempt to address these gaps. You'll notice that it is divided into three parts, each of which is aimed at a different level of your organization.

Although they seem to have different audiences, they belong together as a whole.

The first part makes our best case for data-driven decision-making. Although of interest to any reader, it is primarily aimed at people in senior management positions. These are the decision-makers who don't do the analysis and don't need to understand the methods in detail, but need to be on board and directing the enterprise toward maximizing investment in data. We offer advice on how to build an analytics team, preferably from among existing employees, but we also talk about what to look for in new hires.

The second part is more focused on the people who will be working with data. Few employers in the nonprofit sector can hire statisticians and analysts with advanced degrees, so we have written this section with one person in mind: the math-phobic absolute beginner. We discuss some of the foundational skills required for working with data, which have more to do with concepts than numbers, and nothing to do with equations. We work through basic issues such as getting the data, what to ask for, and what operations to perform on it (regardless of software).

Too many normal, non-geeky people have somehow been convinced that working with data is not for them. We have faith, however, that although not everyone will become an analyst, many unsuspecting people have an innate aptitude for quantitative reasoning that is waiting to be awakened by a clearly explained example that is relevant to their daily work.

That's exactly what you'll find in Part 3 of this book. In this final section, we provide examples of useful and common data analyses that we've done. Every study in this section is something that readers can attempt to reproduce with their own data. Our aim is to impart the "feel" of the essentials of data analysis. Once you have that, there is no limit to what you might do with further reading and study and, above all, playing with your own data.

In short, this is a "whole organization" book, of interest to senior management and aspiring data practitioners alike. It's a trove of ammunition and ideas for anyone desiring to pull their nonprofit or advancement office into the Age of Data.

This is also a nontechnical book, for the most part. We'd like to draw you into a conversation, not bore or confuse you. So we'll take you down a few informal or personal side-roads which may seem only tangentially related to analytics. You may skip these as digressions (they're clearly marked), but we hope you'll come along for the whole ride.

part 1

BECOMING A DATA-DRIVEN ORGANIZATION

Where We Are, Where We're Going

IT'S DIFFICULT TO SAY to what extent development and advancement offices are adopting data-driven methods in planning, decision-making, and day-to-day operations. We can hope that things are improving. But from our vantage point, the sector has a long way to go.

What's holding us back? The conservative nature of our institutions, a natural preference for intuition and narrative over data and analysis, a skills shortage, a fear of disruptive change, skepticism about the claims made for algorithms, a lack of time and resources—we can think of a few answers to that question. Whatever the combination of reasons, our sector is woefully behind where it could be, and should be.

The obvious solution would be for institutional leaders to one day roll out of bed with a fresh mania for plowing mountains of money into analytics while casting aside any doubts about return on investment. Not likely to happen!

Far more likely is the scenario we have both seen and lived: The happy coincidence of an engaged employee with an interest in data and a little time on her hands, working for a decision-maker who has an inkling that this dabbling could lead to something important that changes the game. Bringing the two players in this coincidence closer together is the purpose of this book.

chapter 1

There Has to Be a Better Way

Perhaps you recognize your own institution among the following scenarios.

Your annual fund goes through the same motions every year, sending out oodles of mail at great expense in hopes more people will respond and open their wallets. Staff pin their hopes on an improving economy and other external effects—the tides that are purported to lift all boats. Their mail house has convinced them they need to mail thousands and thousands of non-donors in order to convert a few more each year, at abysmal participation rates. You know that new-donor acquisition is important for the long-term health of the fund, but you also have a nagging sense that mail is going out indiscriminately.

Your prospect researchers are faced with the task of identifying prospects from a pool of tens of thousands of names, using a limited set of criteria for putting names forward for preliminary qualification and assignment. A few years ago, your office spent a lot of money on a wealth screening, which paid off, up to a point. It's dawned on you that wealth does not automatically translate into a gift for your institution; the prospective donor has to like you! You intuit that the key to filling in the "affinity" side of the equation is not "out there" in the world of external wealth and demographic data, but within the homey confines of your own database. No one is looking there, however, and you're not even sure if the data is available, or what kinds of data would be most valuable to have. In the meantime, that capacity data is getting old and you need to make a decision.

Your major gift development officers routinely carry 200 or more prospects in their portfolios—one person has 500! They know a lot of these people quite well, but have to admit that most of the others are complete unknowns aside from their giving histories. They don't know who to call on next, having no criteria by which to prioritize their approaches. One development officer tried to ask the prospect research office for profiles on everyone, and got put in his place! That's not what prospect research does anymore, he was told—it takes a visit to qualify a prospect, and only after qualification will research produce a more complete picture to guide cultivation. Uncertain what to do and reluctant to let prospects go, fundraisers allow them to languish, untouched. Some of them are alumni who have been held out of the annual fund appeal, since they're now prospects for major giving. No one is cultivating them, and they drift away, unknown and unsolicited.

Your planned giving program is growing, but only very slowly. More new expectancies come in as a result of getting a surprise call from an executor than they do as a result of actual cultivation of good prospects. And who knows what a good prospect is to begin with? Your planned giving officers have been focusing almost exclusively on the oldest alumni who have been lifelong loyal donors, with some success. But you have a nagging sense that they ought to be broaching the subject with alumni who are a little younger, perhaps the ones who are looking forward to retirement and are making long-range plans with the help of a financial planner. You also know that a personal approach will yield results; this isn't the type of thing that a mass mailing is going to work on. Unfortunately, you face the same issue that prospect research does: tens of thousands of names, and no clear indication of the best way to proceed.

Your alumni office has sunk serious cash into a wide-ranging survey of alumni. The vendor provided a summary gloss of the results, which the president cherry-picked for those bits that can be interpreted as good news, and now the communications and marketing folks have issued a glowing press release. You imagine that there must be some useful insights locked in there, but no one has the time or skills to find them—and we mean that literally: The binder of reports and the CD with the data have sat on the shelf for so long, no one remembers where they are. Oops!

In short, your institution is spending money at a prodigious rate, and you're not sure whether it's an investment or a waste. Whether all of it is true, or just some of it, you know one thing is for sure: There has got to be a better way.

We see institutions as falling somewhere on this ladder or continuum of competence in analytics, which begins with the most analysis-poor and reaches up to the most analysis-rich organizations:

1. The data needed for analysis does not exist.
2. The data exists but it is not accessible.
3. Data is accessible but no one knows how to analyze it.
4. Someone knows how to analyze it but that person isn't effectively communicating what she's learned.
5. The analyst is communicating but his insights are not being fed into the decision-making process.
6. The analyst's insights sometimes support a decision now and then, on an ad-hoc basis.
7. Analysis is conducted as a regular process, not just ad hoc, but only in one branch or office of the organization. Benefits are realized unevenly across the organization.
8. Data analysis is a normal step in decision-making at all levels (where it has insights to contribute), and benefits are realized across the entire organization.

An unfortunately large number of institutions, large and small, are either at the bottom of this ladder or stuck somewhere in the middle. Rather few aspire to the top two levels. Over the course of this book we hope to help decision-makers and staff workers at each level in their attempt to reach higher.

Intuition Versus Data

In a world that increasingly runs on data and the interpretation of data, university advancement and nonprofit work still tends to follow a combination of gut instinct, intuition, experience, and methods that have worked in the past. The organization may be successful at reporting general results on a quarterly or annual basis, but conducting analyses that address specific business problems is still a foreign concept. In assessing whether some initiative or other is working, the only evidence mustered is nearly always anecdotal and vague.

Intuition has served our species very well. Unfortunately, though, our gut instincts are frequently wrong about specific facts, even very simple facts from our everyday experience. For example, people's sense of elapsed time is quite elastic and inaccurate. Here's what Kevin has to say.

Do you ride the bus back and forth to work? I do. Some days it's a quick trip, and other days it seems to take forever. There's this one stop where the driver will park the bus and just sit there, as the minutes tick by. How dare she! Doesn't she know I'm in a hurry?

I started gathering some data on bus trips in order to figure out which bus (7:15, 7:30, 7:45, etc.) had the most predictable time of arrival at the stop closest to my house, had the lowest variability in travel times, and was the least full (so I would be most likely able to sit down). I thought there might be some optimal combination of these three, but it wasn't evident just from riding the bus. There didn't seem to be any discernable pattern, but yet it could not be just random.

What I found out had less to do with the bus route than with the nature of perceived reality: What you think is going on isn't necessarily what's actually happening.

Over several months, I recorded my twice-daily travel times, from the moment I boarded to the moment I landed on the sidewalk at my destination. Leaving out one extreme outlier, my average trip duration (in either direction) was 38 minutes. So how much did individual trips vary from 38 minutes? Well, 79% of all trips varied from the average by three minutes or less. Three whole minutes! Allow just one more minute of variance, and 90% of trips fit in that window.

So I can hop on any Number 80 bus during rush hour and expect to get to my destination in 38 minutes, give or take a couple of minutes. That's a far cry from how I perceived my commuting time: Some quick rides, some unbearably long ones. In fact, they're all about the same. The bus driver is not trying to drive me crazy by parking the bus in mid-trip; she's ahead of schedule and needs to readjust so commuters farther down the line don't miss their bus.

If we can get simple things wrong, think of all the other assumptions we make about complex stuff, assumptions that could be either confirmed or discarded via a little measuring and analysis. Again and again in this book, we will give examples of insights about alumni and donors that are completely invisible to intuition and could only have been uncovered through analysis, and sometimes insights that are counter to what intuition might tell us.

We are not wrong to have beliefs about how stuff works, but we are wrong in clinging to beliefs when the answers are waiting there in the data.

The Emerging Role of the Analyst

Most fundraisers, alumni officers, and others working in the real world of university advancement do not think of themselves as data workers. If anything, the most effective people in those roles probably characterize themselves as good storytellers. When we communicate with prospective donors or reach out to alumni, we do well to evoke feelings and emotions and go light on the facts. We may attempt to persuade and beguile with numbers and charts that describe how great we are, but that approach will never work as well as one true and powerful story, conveyed in word and image.

But what about the stories we tell to ourselves? Humans need narratives to make sense of the world, but our inborn urge to order events as "this happened, then that happened" leads us into all kinds of unsupported or erroneous assumptions, often related to causation.

How many times have you heard assertions such as "The way to reach young alumni donors is online, because that's where they spend all their time"? Or "We shouldn't ask young alumni to give more than $20, because they have big student loans to pay." Or "There's no need to look beyond loyal donors to find the best prospects for planned giving." Or "We should stop calling people for donations, because focus groups say they don't like to get those calls."

Such mini-narratives are all around us, and we all too frequently rely on them when dealing with the scenarios presented at the beginning of this chapter. Who knows whether they're true or not? They might make intuitive sense, or they're told to us by people with experience. Experts tell us stories like this. Donor surveys and reports on philanthropic trends tell stories, too. And we act on them, not because we know they're true, but because we believe them.

Strictly speaking, no assumption can be "true" in the sense that it applies everywhere and at all times. Making assertions about causation in connection with complex human behaviors such as philanthropy or engagement is suspect right from the start. Even when there is some truth, whose truth is it? Trend watchers and experts who know nothing about your constituency are going to lead you astray with their suppositions.

There is a scene in the movie *Moneyball* in which one grizzled baseball scout says a certain player must lack confidence "because his girlfriend is ugly." We can hope that most received wisdom about advancement is not as embarrassingly stupid, but the logic should be familiar.

The 2011 movie, based on the book of the same name by Michael Lewis, tells the story of Billy Beane (played by Brad Pitt), the general manager of the Oakland A's in the late 1990s, who needed to field a winning team on a meager payroll. Beane and his assistant general manager Paul DePodesta had an idea: There had to be champion players out there whom everyone else had overlooked; if no one was looking for them, they would be affordable. Their prospecting tool would be statistical analysis. For example, their analysis showed that new stats such as on-base percentage and slugging percentage were better predictors of offensive success than the tried-and-true qualities valued by traditional buyers of talent. The analytical approach paid off, and it was soon copied by other major league baseball teams.

The movie didn't have much to do with analytics, but had some great lines that translate well from the baseball field to the analytics field. This one, for example: "Your goal shouldn't be to buy players," the character based on DePodesta says to Beane. "Your goal should be to buy wins. In order to buy wins, you need to buy runs."

It's a statement about success with statistical modeling: You have to start by properly framing the question. The rest is just technique. The analytical approach doesn't pay off for professional sports like it used to, because now everyone does it. (The Oakland A's have not been as successful since.) But analytics will always pay off in the nonprofit world because in the hunt for potential donors we still mostly compete against ourselves. We either identify our friends and supporters effectively, or we don't.

The antidote to being led astray in your line of work is learning what's actually true about your own donors and your own constituency. It's a new world: We've got the tools and the smarts to put any assertion to the test, in the environment of our own data. The age of basing decisions on fact instead of supposition has arrived.

No doubt some feel threatened by that. We can imagine a time when something like observation-driven, experimental medicine started to break on the scene. Doctors treating mental illness by knocking holes in peoples' skulls to let out the bad spirits must have resisted the tide. The witch doctors, and the baseball scouts obsessed with ugly girlfriends, may have had a lot of experience, but does anyone miss them?

The role of the analyst is *not* to shut down our natural, storytelling selves. No. The role of the analyst is to treat every story as a hypothesis. Not in order to explode it necessarily, but to inject validity, context, and relevance. The role of the analyst, in short, is to help us tell better and better stories.

It's Still About People

Let's be clear about who the master storytellers are in your organization. They are your frontline fundraisers, alumni officers, student recruiters, and anyone else with a job that requires them to be outward-facing. They may be dealing primarily with alumni, friends of the university, volunteers, donors, and prospective donors, or with people and organizations from the surrounding community.

What happens to those roles when the organizational culture shifts toward data-driven decision-making? Well, nothing really. A culture of analytics is meant to serve these roles, not subsume them. An experienced frontline fundraiser might feel vaguely threatened by this whole data mining thing, like the witch doctor of old. That person might wonder, Does experience not count for anything? Is gut instinct now a fundraising tool of the past? Are all our ideas about how fundraising works in danger of being supplanted by some computer-generated mumbo-jumbo?

In a word, no. Data mining is exciting, powerful, and new to many of us, but its arrival at your organization will not displace or invalidate anything you've come to know about how, for example, to best ask for a gift when you're sitting face-to-face with the prospective donor in her living room. It complements your strategy; it does not replace it. Fundraising and friend-raising are still all about relationships. They will always be about relationships.

We could go even further and say that frontline fundraisers are the real miners in the organization. Data miners are more like exploration geologists, pointing out the areas that might yield the most gold. "Dig here," says the data miner to the fundraiser. "This ore body is likely to contain what you're looking for." And the fundraiser does the hard work, digging through the rock to find the nuggets within, using the same qualification tools he or she has always used: experience, personal contact, intuition.

The fundraiser can find gold without the data miner. But it's not easy. He or she will dig anywhere, sinking dozens of useless shafts before striking a workable vein. Or maybe the fundraiser is into dowsing or using amulets or crystals or something similarly occult to decide where to dig. That's worked before. Not well, mind you. As they say, even a stopped clock is right twice a day. What predictive modeling does is help bring fundraiser and would-be donor together by increasing the odds (sometimes dramatically) that the meeting of minds will successfully converge on a gift.

The data miner, on the other hand, is useless without the fundraiser, or the alumni officer, or whoever the end user of knowledge might be. Insight without action gets nowhere. Marry the two, though, and you've got a powerful force. No one's skills become obsolete—the fundraiser still needs all his or her "traditional" knowledge while digging. Only now, the chances that the digging will earn a return on investment are vastly improved.

What characterizes a fruitful relationship between these two camps is a sense of boundaries, a willingness to cooperate, and a certain amount of faith in methods employed by the other. The data miner may not really grasp the art of asking for a gift or organizing a reunion, and doesn't need to. The fundraiser may not grasp the science of segmenting the prospect pool for propensity to give, and doesn't need to. Both sides can learn more about what the other does, but it's more important that each treat the other's domain of knowledge with respect.

Fundraisers already work in a profession that refers to human beings as "prospects" and "suspects"—pseudo-sales terminology we would be glad to see dispensed with. To some, sticking scores and labels on people must seem like an extension of a clinical mindset that likes nothing more than bar-coding, profiling, and commodifying people as if they were widgets. Maybe we can be so busy studying our numbers and charts that we lose our connection with the donor, and with our mission.

We don't think so.

What Are We Trying to Do?

When we talk about predictive modeling to an audience that knows nothing about it, here's what we say:

> Predictive modeling allows us to adjust our strategy according to
> differences among individuals.

That's a far cry from treating human beings as only numbers!

In the regular brand of fundraising that the majority of our institutions conduct, the characteristic of our constituents that we are primarily concerned with is giving history, or lack of it. We may consider the college or faculty of the alum's degree when we make our approach, and sometimes the age of the alum, but mostly our strategy is driven by giving history. This is not true of the cultivation and solicitation stages in major gift fundraising, of course, but its earliest stage (prospect identification) is often all about giving history.

This obsession with past giving means that everyone in the database ends up being classified into a few huge categories. The labels for these categories are familiar: non-donors, lapsed donors, major donors, "last year but unfortunately not this" (LYBUNTs), "some year but …" (SYBUNTs), and so on. No matter how sophisticated our segmentation based on these categories, our approach is one-size-fits-all for the majority of prospects: acquisition, renewal, reactivation, and upgrading.

How many people gave $25 to your institution last year? Thousands, potentially. Are they all equally likely to give $50 next year? Of course not, but a look at our solicitation strategy would indicate that we think they are.

What percentage of your alumni have never given a dime? Fifty percent? Sixty? Are all these non-donors equally likely to be acquired as a new donor this year? Is everyone from last year's graduating class equally likely to make their first gift? Absolutely not, to both questions. The way we spread money around in mailing and phoning this segment, however, seems to indicate that we think they are.

Predictive modeling allows us to take other factors into account. Did the alum play sports as a student? Did he or she live on campus? Has he or she attended a reunion since graduating? Potentially dozens of characteristics can inform our models, allowing us to better discriminate among a sea of prospects. If we work in annual giving, our actual solicitation of prospects may not be any more personal than before—the sheer numbers won't allow it—but we can be much better focused on the people who are most likely to support us.

Can we do all this without resorting to the database? Can we have a relationship with someone without data?

Yes and no. It's a matter of scale. A single human being can maintain only a certain number of relationships before it becomes unmanageable. The number will vary, but it will never exceed a few hundred. For some it will be far fewer.

Think of a planned giving officer faced with a pool of 2,000 potential prospects. Many schools will have that many alumni over the age of 50 or 55 who have giving histories consistent with the conventional notion of what makes a good planned giving prospect. Who among that undifferentiated pool of 2,000 people (just counting alumni) should be approached first? Yes, personal relationships trump a probability model every time. But what officer in the field, or staff of field officers, has met with 2,000 alumni?

Where the numbers and the stats leave off, the art of the personal begins— that's the proper order. No model can capture that emotional and motivating element in philanthropy, but no amount of experience, insight, relationships, or knowledge of trends will allow one gift officer to make a personal connection with thousands of people. Predictive models offer a better than fighting chance that the person the gift officer is calling on will desire that personal connection.

The Unfortunate Reality

In the introduction, we celebrated the fact that now is the perfect time for analytics to bloom in the nonprofit sector. We have cheap computing, user-friendly software, an educated workforce, an exploding amount of available data, and a growing awareness of the power of data. But if analytic practice was growing of its own accord in our sector, there would be no need of this book. The fact is, it's an uphill battle. As a vendor, Peter is on the front lines, and the view from there is not pretty. This next section describes what he sees every week.

What do John Sammis and I see out there in the world of higher education and general nonprofits that puts the brakes on the growth of analytic practice? Here's a partial list of three:

1. Things move slowly in the world of not-for-profits.
2. People who are in positions of authority who should get this stuff, simply don't.
3. There is a high rate of turnover of employees working in advancement.

The Pace

When I think of the pace at which things get done in our sector, I'm reminded of a certain day in August of 1996. Linda and I had rented a cottage in the village of South Sutton, New Hampshire, for the month. Winters in New Hampshire tend to leave the roads looking like a toned-down version of the Grand Canyon when the snow and ice finally depart. That was the case with Route 114, which we used every day both with automobile and with bicycle. Somewhere in the middle of the month a crew of six guys and gals came with dump trucks, steamrollers (that's what they called them when I was a kid), and oversized rakes to fix about six miles of the road. Took 'em about two days to get it done.

I couldn't believe it. As they were packing up, I stopped the car and rolled down the window to address a country boy who looked like he might have been a relative of mine.

"How ya doin'?" I asked.

"Good, and you?"

"Real good. Can I ask ya question?"

"Shooah."

"Can y'all come down to D.C. where I live and fix our roads?"

With a straight face he replied, "Too hot down theah."

That little exchange took place just at the time I was starting to get into the analytics work I do now. As the years have passed I've thought about that day many times. And when I have, I've thought that the pace at which things get done in not-for-profits is like the pace at which road repair gets done where I live in the District of Columbia. Slower (to borrow from an old Spanish expression) than a procession of turtles.

In D.C., public works projects move slowly for a lot of reasons, not the least of which is colossal ineptitude on the part of the officials who let the contracts and oversee the work. But I don't think that's the case in not-for-profits. Sure, there are pockets of incompetence in these institutions, but it's not widespread. I think the primary reason is that there is simply not a sense of *urgency* over getting things done in these places.

The impediment that John Sammis and I encounter most frequently is the huge amount of time it takes the organizations we work with to prepare data for analysis. Here's how it often goes. We agree to do a data-mining and predictive modeling project for the institution. To perform the work we need to have either an Excel or text file constructed from the donor/prospective donor database. At a minimum the file will have 10,000 records and anywhere from 40 to 100 fields. In our view, building the file should take no more than a week if the job is put in the hands of a competent IT staff person.

Sadly, that estimate is woefully optimistic. On average it can take between a month and six months for us to receive the file. Why does it take so long to perform such a straightforward task? We hear all kinds of excuses to which we have to reply with, "That's okay. Get it to us when you can. We're ready when you're ready." That sort of thing.

But when we talk with each other, the essence of what we say is, "What the heck are they doing? If we took that long to get things done, we'd be out of business." And we would.

If you're groaning in agreement with us, you understand. If you're not groaning, that's a good thing. That means you work in a unit where things get done on a timely basis. And you are most assuredly the rare exception.

The Cluelessness

Let's say that you, the reader of this book, are a decision-maker of a certain rank. We are pleased to have your attention and interest. You get it. Given all the hype about data in recent years, you might assume that your counterparts at other institutions also "get it" and that you are playing catch-up. The reality from our view is that you are rather exceptional. You are a decision-maker who recognizes the inestimable value of your institution's data investment, and for that we salute you. But you are a rare bird, and that distresses us. Unfortunately there are plenty of people who hold positions of power and authority who should get this stuff—but don't. A few years back, John Sammis and I wrote a CASE white paper that opened with these paragraphs:

> It was a stifling hot day in Chicago in July of 2007. I was at the CASE Summit looking out at an audience of some 100 folks clearly older than the 30-somethings John Sammis and I regularly work with. After being introduced, I paced back and forth in front of them, not uttering a word for a good 20 seconds. Then I stopped abruptly, peered out at them, and said: "I work with the young professionals who report to you guys. Heads of the annual fund. Directors of prospect research and alumni relations. And those overworked and underpaid IT folks in advancement services.
>
> "With them, I feel I have to be pretty nice. After all, they're in the trenches working away every day trying to keep the fundraising machinery of your schools running as smoothly as they can. But ..."
>
> I paused for a little dramatic effect as frowns and grimaces crawled onto their faces. "But with you guys I can be more blunt and candid. That's part of what you get paid for." The frowns and grimaces hardened. "Here's the deal. If your counterparts in the private sector—and I'm talking mostly people in direct marketing—ignored the meager information they store on their customers the way most of you ignore the vast information you store on your alums, ya know what would happen? They'd go out of business in six months."

A number of years have passed since I put on that little show in front of those vice president types. I often ask myself: "Have things really changed all that much in terms of how these high-level managers are embracing the concept of data-driven decision-making?" I think my answer is that there is some good news, and there is some bad news. Let's start with the bad news. Most decision-makers still allow practices where:

- Huge amounts of money are wasted on mailings and calling,
- Vendors charge high prices for services without providing solid evidence that those services will be worth the expenditure,
- They remain unaware of basic information in their databases, and
- Generous donors go unattended.

Mailing and calling

Call me crazy, but by this point in the 21st century it should be obvious to a manager who oversees any kind of mass calling or mailing program that mailing and calling everybody the same number of times is foolish. Nonetheless, I talk to schools and nonprofits every week where this kind of practice is routinely followed. Expensive alumni magazines are sent out quarterly to tens of thousands of alumni who have never given a penny to the institution and probably never will. All non-donor alums are called at least once even if they have been out of school for more than 15 years and have never made one pledge. No real effort is made to determine costs per mail piece or per call so that some measure of return on investment can be computed.

Vendor services

I don't think it's uncommon for one vendor to say "I'm in the wrong business" when he or she hears about the prices another vendor charges—prices that so far exceed his or her own prices that the comparison is laughable. I know that John and I say that all the time. A comment like that is motivated in part by jealousy and by frustration at our own clumsiness when it comes to pricing. But part of our saying it is motivated by our surprise over how easy it is for vendors to sell advancement products and services without offering strong evidence that those products or services will work or be useful.

I have to be cautious here lest a particular vendor become so obvious that we open ourselves up to litigation. So let me pick an area where the problem is so widespread that no one vendor can possibly feel singled out: web surveys. With the advent of the Internet and its exponential growth over the last decade and a half, web surveys have gained a strong foothold in society in general, and in higher education advancement in particular. These surveys are not cheap. We're not experts on surveys, and certainly not on web surveys. However, let's assume the vendor you use to do a survey emails either a random sample of your alumni (or your entire universe of alumni) and invites them to go to a website and fill out a survey. If they do this, you will encounter the problem of poor response rate. If you're lucky, maybe 30% of the people your vendor emails will respond, even if the vendor follows up and vigorously encourages nonresponders to fill the thing out. Please.

This is a problem. There will always be the lingering question of whether or not the nonresponders are fundamentally different from the responders with respect to what they're being surveyed about. But the larger problem is that too many vice presidents who must approve the purchase of such survey services won't ask the prospective vendor questions like:

"Will responders:

- Give us a far more positive view of our institution than the nonresponders would have?
- Tell us they really like new programs the school is offering, programs the nonresponders may really dislike, or like a lot less than the responders do?
- Offer suggestions for changes in how alumni should be approached— changes that non-responders would not offer or actively discourage?"

Nor will these vice presidents ask the prospective vendor to do some checking to see if the responders:

- Are older or younger than the non-responders,
- Have a higher or lower median lifetime giving than the non-responders,
- Attend more or fewer events after they graduate than the nonresponders, or
- Are more or less likely than the non-responders to be members of a dues-paying alumni association.

Here you may be thinking, "Come on, Pete, aren't you being a bit hard on us? You can't expect us all to be experts in survey research and be automatically poised to ask a whole bunch of penetrating questions like these." I would agree. I probably am being too hard. On the other hand, far too many decision-makers get swept up in the enthusiasm and sizzle of vendor presentations without putting on the brakes to look for holes in the hype.

You can't be expected to find all the holes in the hype, but you ought to ask more questions of vendors that are tied to data. Far too many decision-makers are signing on the dotted line without asking such questions and demanding straightforward answers.

Unaware of the basics
I never stop being amazed at how little vice presidents of advancement know about the information in their databases, especially their alumni databases. How much do YOU know? For example, do you know what percentage of your solicitable alums have:

- Ever given you any money at all?
- Given you more than $50 lifetime?
- An email address listed in the database?
- A business phone number listed in the database?

The honest vice presidents will almost always answer these with, "I really don't know." Then the question becomes: *Should* you know the answers to these questions? I think you should, but I'm more than a little biased.

Unfortunately, too many high-level managers blithely assume they know things about their alumni that they don't know. I can't tell you the number of times I've heard stories about some new vice president who pronounces that a major giving prospect for the next campaign can only be someone who has already given a single gift of greater than $100,000. And what do those vice presidents do when they learn that there are no more than five people in the database who meet that criterion? I'm not sure. I hope they say, "Gee, what else should I know about these folks that I don't know?"

The Turnover

My father went to work for General Electric in 1928; he retired in 1971. Forty-three years. Only real job he ever had. Well, you don't need me to tell you that those days of long-term employment in North America are gone. Look at yourself and look at the people around you. How long have you been working at the same job in the same institution, and how long have they been there? And what effect does this churn have on getting data-driven decision-making to sink its teeth into the advancement culture of higher education institutions and nonprofits? Here's what we too often see:

- **We agree to do a data-mining/predictive modeling project with a staff member or members at an institution**. Maybe the project involves our training staff to do modeling for themselves. Maybe the project involves our building several models for the institution. Maybe the project involves some combination of the two. Whatever the circumstances, the staff members are usually enthused and energetic about what we will be doing with and for them.

- **We complete the project**. These projects usually extend over a number of months and end with a commitment on the part of the staff to use the products (almost always a set of scores) to save money and generate more revenue on appeals.

- **We follow up with the institution, or someone from the institution contacts us**. Whichever of these two things happens, about a year has passed since we finished the project.

- **Everybody we originally worked with has left the institution**. Hard to believe? We think so, too. It doesn't happen every week, but it does happen more than you might expect.

And the consequences of this scenario? It's way worse than losing all the data you never backed up on your laptop.

The Good News

So much for the bad news. Let's talk about some good news. In recent years some things have happened that have caused John Sammis and Peter to feel a bit more heartened about the future for analytics in higher education advancement, in particular the way higher level leaders in advancement are starting to embrace data-driven decision-making. Here's Peter's list:

- At a nationally recognized private higher ed institution west of the Mississippi, we had an extended conference call to talk about a data-mining project. On that call were two senior vice presidents who were more animated about the project than the people under them who had gotten the ball rolling in the first place. We couldn't see the faces of these troupers, but we suspect they were smiling contentedly. And we suspect they were saying to themselves, "This is good. This is what we need. Finally, the stone is rolling downhill rather than our having to grunt and groan to push it uphill."

- We had a conversation with the head of the annual fund and the top advancement executive at a public higher ed school about a predictive model building project. Since the annual fund head is such a delightful character, the VP hung back a bit and sort of enjoyed the banter between John, me, and her very capable employee. But every now and then the VP would guffaw or add a word or two of support or ask a penetrating question that taxed John's and my ability to answer it. And what a breath of fresh air that whole experience was.

- A vice president who heads up advancement at a small Midwestern college contacted us about a project that would involve some training of her staff. In our initial discussion with her, we made it clear that the success of the training and its enduring effect on the advancement culture at the college would depend heavily on her active support. She said: "I plan to sit in on all the training sessions." She kept her word. I can't tell you the impact that had on us and, more important, on her staff.

Kevin:

What Peter has observed, I have experienced. When I was beginning to get interested in data mining as a prospect researcher, it was a personal interest. I figured data mining had to have applications for my work, otherwise I would not have pursued it, but it was up to me to discover those applications and then do the work. Data mining was a new idea in our department, but I was fortunate in that our vice president was unusually receptive to trying new things, especially if it involved making intelligent use of data. We obtained some training, and I fit data mining around my other tasks.

In time, the vice president left to join another university. Not coincidentally, I followed about a year later, to work in the annual fund in his department. My previous employer had given me much—the freedom to play with our data and to learn as much as I could about analytics. But this larger university had a bigger database and an even more pressing need for predictive analytics; it was no further ahead than the university I had left. So there was a lot of good, challenging work to do. Most important, however, I knew that the leadership of my new employer was foursquare behind data-driven decision-making. Instead of being left alone to putter around with personal data projects, I would be responsible for building models for real deployment.

Two years after changing employers, my position has evolved into a mix of business analysis for our department, including the alumni office, and predictive modeling. What was once an absorbing extracurricular interest is now my full-time job—a development for which I am extremely grateful. It should be noted that I can't take credit for making it my job. I sought to develop my own skills (often on my own time), but it was my employer who recognized that we had a need for analytics and that there was someone in the department who could grow into a role that filled the need.

These good-news stories have a common theme, in which two elements come together to make something happen. The first element is an engaged employee who is keen on doing innovative work with data and who makes a personal investment of time and attention in learning skills. The second is a decision-maker who understands the importance of doing this work and who is able to recognize that person among his or her employees who can be encouraged and developed to meet the challenge.

We wish this happy coincidence were the norm, but unfortunately it is not. Our goal with this book is to bring these two elements closer together. We want to encourage data-interested employees to pursue their explorations, but also to keep institutional goals in mind when they do so. And, on the other side, we want to help decision-makers learn what traits to look for as they build the capacity for analytics on their team.

chapter 2

Building a Culture of Analytics

In our observation, the initial move in the direction of beefing up strength in analytics has not come from the top. It's come from the staffers who attend conferences, read books and blogs on their weekends, and conduct side-projects on their own initiative. They may be prospect researchers or work in annual giving, but they have one thing in common: They're not the ones in charge. If they're lucky, they have the freedom to use some of what they've learned in their work. But it's not enough—that does not make data-driven decision-making part of the culture.

What about the people who ARE in charge? What are they doing? Are they shouting from the rooftops:

- that data-driven decision-making is a way to make a significant dent in their huge pool of alumni non-donors?

- that data-driven decision-making is a way to stop wasting hundreds of thousands of dollars on mailing costs and calling costs associated with their annual fund reach-outs?

- that data-driven decision-making is the way to find new major giving prospects who may be on the verge of making some substantial gifts but who won't ever be asked unless they are uncovered by our kind of analysis?

- that there is huge potential in the data they already have at their electronic fingertips and how utterly foolish they are to allow vendors to sell them costly products and services that essentially ignore the powerful internal data?

- that (unless they are very small) they must invest in the hiring and/ or training of staff who can ultimately analyze the hell out of their own data because no vendor (regardless of how competent and well-intentioned) can possibly stay on top of their data the way an in-house person/team can?

Some of you in charge who are reading this book may be able to answer yes to some of these questions. Unfortunately, the answer to each of these questions is almost always NO.

In a data-driven organization, the culture runs from top to bottom. Everyone gets it. In our heads we carry an image of what the ideal organization looks like. The advancement/development leader of your institution is fully committed to data-driven decision-making. It's not an option. Directors and managers are made to understand that it's part of the job. You either start paying attention to the data in the way you run your show or you find another line of work. Maybe we don't throw you out of the organization, but you will no longer oversee budgets that waste huge amounts of money on fundraising efforts that are not driven by data.

There is an in-house quant team (to begin with, that could be but one person) whose job it is to serve all the major fundraising constituencies (major giving askers, prospect research, call center, etc.). These folks are charged with the tasks of:

- Constantly interviewing their in-house customers about their needs (predictive scores for making contact; predictive scores for snail mail appeals, predictive scores for event attendance; the list goes on and on),
- Building models that generate scores,
- Helping customers get those scores into a usable format,
- Advising customers on how best to use scores in concert with currently established segmentation techniques,
- Assessing the effectiveness of the scores on appeals, and improving models for the next round, and
- Providing honest but diplomatic regular reports to top management on the degree to which the in-house customers are using and benefiting from their services.

Building from Within

How then do directors and vice presidents go about building an in-house team of analysts? Perhaps we instinctively think of going out to the marketplace to hire talent with the statistical and research chops to fit the bill. But there might be a better way.

Using in-house talent, the people who are already working for you, is usually better than finding someone from outside. Hiring someone externally takes time and resources that you don't have to expend when you promote or transfer someone who already works for you.

The sad truth is that outside talent often doesn't work out. Perhaps it's not a fair comparison, but look at how badly educational institutions botch the job of hiring new vice presidents and presidents. Perhaps organizations look outside so often because the in-house candidates have all their warts and pimples showing (as well as their many strengths). The outside candidates (in terms of references and in the glow of the short-list interviews) look radiant, pure as the driven snow. And then … two months or so into the job … they don't look quite the same. In fact, they often look more flawed than the acne-faced internal candidate who was passed over. Many in higher education can relate to this phenomenon.

Internal candidates know your institution. They know how the database works or they know the go-to people who can fix something that isn't working. They know the capable folks in advancement, and they know the ones who are on active retirement or, worse, roadblocks who should be avoided at all costs. They know your alumni. You can't assume that about an outsider. If the person comes from a hoity-toity school, he or she may have a condescending view of your largely commuter-student population made up of those who weren't high school valedictorians or graduates of St. Paul's or Exeter.

Good internal candidates have already shown you they are keen on data-driven decision-making. At staff meetings they bring up the wealth of internal data you have on alums that gets ignored when you plan call and mail appeals or ramp up a campaign. They bemoan the cost of expensive outside vendors who talk a good game but don't deliver products and services that save money and generate more revenue on appeals. They cajole, beg, or beseech you to let them go to seminars and conferences where they can learn more about analytics, in spite of your constant refrain: "We just don't have the budget for that." They send you links to articles and blogs that make a strong case for internal analytics. They even bring you the results of mini analyses they've done in Excel that show that they may well like analysis better than their "day job."

Not every possible candidate is raising her hand, though. In fact, the best person for the job might not even be aware of his own aptitude for analytical work. But there are keeners in every organization, and there are ways to spot them. They may not come with all the skills, but in their curiosity they are poised for growth.

Anyone with the right attitude could be a good pick. That person just needs your help.

Identifying and Developing In-House Talent

Perhaps you're looking around your offices and not seeing anyone who might fit the bill of an innovator. True, the skill level probably isn't there for many organizations. But skills are not the limiting factor. Some training, and not necessarily expensive training, even for the one-on-one variety, might be enough to address a shortage of skills.

The quality you're looking for is **aptitude.** Working in this field does seem to require a certain type of mind. Not a mathematical mind necessarily, but a mind that feeds on concepts, a mind that is creative and always curious about the measurable, the quantifiable, the comparable—and often a good deal more. An aptitude for analytics may not be acquirable in the way a regular skill is, but it can be discovered, developed, and fostered. If you are an employer or someone else responsible for managing employees whom you wish to encourage in this direction, here are five elements that are important for getting there. Some of these elements are things to watch for that will help identify good candidates for analytical work. Others are for fostering that talent once you've identified it.

1. Time for personal projects

You may be familiar with the example of Google, famous for requiring that its engineers spend 20% of their time working on personal technology projects unrelated to their primary projects. You probably use a few of the free resources that have resulted from that practice. We don't see nonprofits ever going that far, but some version of the idea might be possible. Is there a down time in your year? Maybe only one or two employees out of 10 will have the mindset for independent, creative work that will allow them to make use of unstructured time. Probably all you can do is provide some shelter for this development to take place. During relatively quiet periods, don't assign busy work to creative people, and don't insist that they take vacation only during those times.

2. An eye on business problems

Your employees' personal projects will be exploratory and research-based, but they ought to be tethered to your real business problems and fundraising goals. Those problems and goals are embedded in your organization's (or department's) annual plan. You must have some sort of annual plan, first of all, and communicate it to employees. Encourage thinking about how to reach goals.

3. Interesting challenges

Juggling the politically sensitive seating arrangements for 400 guests for a gala dinner is a challenge, but is it interesting? A creative person might find the challenge interesting the first time, but unless he or she can figure out a way to automate the process somehow, the task will quickly turn to drudgery. The natural analyst among your employees is the one who asks, "Is there a better way to do this?" If you're the boss, recognize that you've got two types of employees, both valuable. The first type is the one who carries out predetermined processes (juggling seat assignments for the gala), and the second type is the one who actually designs or changes those processes. The first type gets the work done; the second type defines what work looks like in the future. Innovation is designing new and better ways to get work done. As an employer, one of the best tasks to give a creative worker is, "Find a better way to do this."

4. Reaching outside the organization

For the majority of organizations, the data analyst will be a lone wolf; few institutions will enjoy the luxury of having a whole team of analysts. Other employees might be able to discuss work issues in detail due to their shared body of knowledge, but your budding analyst might stand alone—not learning, not growing, not as alert to what is happening in the field. This person needs to cultivate professional connections outside your own group. Fortunately, at no time in history has this been more possible; the Internet has made distance irrelevant. As the boss, you should encourage networking outside the organization, or at least don't discourage it. This includes making the investment in sending employees to conferences, signing up for webinars, paying for memberships in professional organizations, and (most important for data mining) investing in one-on-one training. Are employees with external connections more likely to leave? Probably not. The benefits of allowing talented employees to acquire what they need to do their jobs effectively (and therefore, with more satisfaction) outweighs the risk of having them network their way to their next job. Keep an eye out for the employees who take advantage of these opportunities.

5. Identify communicators

To become an advocate for data-driven decision-making in your organization from top to bottom, you don't have to understand analytic practice in detail. You will, however, need to call on your would-be analysts to explain their work. Repeatedly! As the boss, you can preach the gospel of analytics all you want, but a data-mining effort may fail in the application simply because the people who ought to be using the scores aren't, for whatever reason. Maybe they don't understand the concepts, maybe they're uncomfortable with an approach driven by numbers instead of intuition. Don't assume that they're at fault for not "getting it." Consider that it's your analyst employee's job to educate others about the practice and aims of analytics. He needs to be capable of doing presentations to staff, circulate interesting findings in readable prose, and meet face-to-face to argue the case for making better use of data. Do you have regular staff meetings that employees may use as a venue for discussing their work? It's wonderful if you can be an advocate for data-driven decision-making yourself, but your creative employee should also always be ready to explain what she's up to.

Some of these pointers offer characteristics to look for in your employees, while others will require employees to stretch a bit. For example, it's very likely that your would-be analyst is not an outgoing, Type A communicator. Not to put too much emphasis on stereotypes, but it's probably true that most analytical workers would rather operate behind the scenes than on the stage. Never mind. If they have a passion for their work, they will desire to communicate it. (Believe us—we've been there.) They will stretch toward this new challenge. Just be aware that you *will* need them to make that stretch, or else your chances of success will be diminished.

Should You Hire Instead?

If you would like to have someone on your staff devoted full-time (or pretty much so) to a data-mining position, we've already made a strong case for finding someone who works at your institution. "But," you say, "that's not gonna work. We simply don't have anyone on board who comes close to meeting the criteria you guys have laid out for us. We've got to go to the outside."

We've thought about what we would do were we in your shoes. You may not particularly like the first step we suggest: deciding whether you and your institution are *ready* to hire a motivated and talented person.

Peter has the stronger feelings on this matter, so let's have him express his thoughts:

I have been working as a consultant for almost 35 years, and I have been exposed to all kinds of organizations over that period. Frankly, there are precious few of those organizations where I would have encouraged anyone to pursue a job or accept a job offer. It's not that those organizations were worse places to work for than organizations that did not avail themselves of my services. Not at all. If anything, the organizations I've consulted to were more, not less, employee friendly than the ones that would never have hired me and my colleagues. So what I have to say is not encouraging.

Let's start with gender. In this book we're addressing a field that is two-thirds female, one-third male. The first thing I'd like to ask our readers is this: What are you doing to make the professional lives of your female employees more satisfying and less frustrating? When I ask that question, it is with several things in mind. Let's start with remuneration. The CASE Salary Survey consistently shows that female advancement employees make, on average, about $10,000 less than their male counterparts—that is, men who are roughly the same age, have been at the institution the same amount of time, have the same level of managerial responsibility, and on and on the list goes. That it is outrageous, and it is correctable.

Another biggie for women who have young children (and there are oodles of them in advancement) is telecommuting. If you're a mother of children under 10 (just to pick a number), wouldn't you like to be able to work from home at least two days a week and avoid that enervating commute and all those endless meetings and save the environment from some of the pollution your car emits on its 10 hours back and forth to work every week? Not just mothers of young children, but any employees doing knowledge work who don't need to be on-site five days a week, would answer in the affirmative.

The next thing I'd mention is leadership, the person at the helm of the organization, such as the president of a college or university, or the chief executive officer of a general nonprofit. Some of them are gifted leaders. Inspiring. Well-liked by employees and members and students and alumni. They're like precious gems. And the rest? Mediocre at best, downright toxic at worst.

I have to be careful here because I don't want to make anyone's job worse than it already is, but I have a good friend in mind. By the time this book comes out she will no longer be working for this extremely prestigious nonprofit, all because of a boss who insults his employees in front of other people. She has put this guy on notice: If he ever does it again to her, she will walk out the door and leave him holding the bag with a campaign that she has been doing a masterful job of running.

Fortunately, I think this guy is atypical. I don't think most CEOs openly demean their employees. But they can demotivate the troops in other ways. I know an extremely talented annual fund director who is leaving a place he loves because the president of the school is ... can I say "an idiot"? He insists on reading and approving all the many mail pieces my friend sends out to alumni. He adds in big words where small words would be better, disparages the use of contractions, that sort of thing. Kevin, who is more polite, would call him a micromanager. Maybe if the guy were just a low-level supervisor I'd call him that, but he's the president of a prestigious college. He's an idiot.

The question I have for readers is: Given the current leadership in your organization (and what it is likely to be over the next several years), can you in good conscience bring someone in who has a chance to really flourish in the job? You don't have to give a firm answer to the question, but you do have to think hard about what your honest answer might be.

Let's talk for a second about you, the prospective boss for this person you want to hire. There are tons of books on being a boss. I even wrote one of them, long, long ago. There's no harm in reading books on how to improve your management skills. But that's not the central issue. The central issue is whether or not you're the kind of a boss a new hire would want to work for. I think the process for answering the question is straightforward, but executing the process is hard because it can be very threatening.

I'm suggesting you arrange to meet with the following people individually for an hour: two of your employees (and one has to be one you don't get along with all that well), your boss, your spouse or significant other, and your best friend. Before you actually sit down with the person, give each one a general sense of why you want to meet. When you do meet, somewhere where you won't be disturbed for an hour, you say something like this:

"Terry, I'm going to ask you to give me some frank feedback on my role as a boss. I value what you have to say, so please don't hold back. Be candid. I'd like you to start with the things you think I do well as a boss. Then I want you to tell me three things I could do to be a better boss. While you talk, my body language and my eye contact will be open and receptive. Most important, I will never interrupt you and offer my thoughts or reactions to what you're telling me. If you stop talking I will remain quiet. At the very most I might say, 'Keep going. I need to hear this.'"

Most people, especially non-stop talkers (and there are just so many of them out there who are bosses), will struggle mightily with the process. It would be difficult for anyone to not interrupt and turn the thing into a conversation, or even a debate. But I'd like our readers who are bosses to give it a try. I think they'll benefit hugely from the effort, and they'll get themselves a lot closer to deciding whether they are ready to bring on a data miner whom they won't immediately demotivate and make regret the decision to take the job.

Not a typical approach to bringing on a new hire, to be sure. But consider that if you do intend to hire externally, you must be looking for a certain level of education, credentials, experience, and proven skill. Otherwise, why hire? You might be willing to make investments in the growth of a current employee, but a new employee has to bring the goods. Unfortunately for you, people with these specialized skills are in demand in every sector. As a nonprofit, you may not be able to afford your ideal candidate, so at a minimum you have to offer a work environment that is worth making the move for: one that is a good place for anyone, but amenable to women in particular (analysts in this field are very likely to be female), and one where the leadership is a rudder and not an anchor. Your analytics hire is not in charge, but he or she will be helping to guide decisions from top to bottom in the organization—because if not, why are you hiring an analyst? Someone with the skills and experience, and the desire to make a difference, will not long work in an organization in which her insights are ignored or twisted to suit an agenda. Not when there are greener pastures in all directions.

Finding (and Wooing) the Right Fit

Let's assume you've satisfied yourself that both you and the institution you work for are ready to bring in a new hire to do data mining and predictive modeling. More specifically, you're satisfied that the new person won't arrive on the scene and shortly decide that she's made a big mistake and that she should have stayed right where she was before you ever contacted her.

Fair enough. How do you go about finding someone like that? There is no one best answer to this question. And, more important, there is a good chance that the person you eventually hire will not be even close to the ideal candidate you're seeking.

Why do we say that? Think about your own experience in the world of work. Think about all the new hires who have come on board in the places you've worked throughout your professional life. How many of them looked terrific on paper and seemed darn good when they came in for the interview? But how many of all those folks ended up working out really well in the new job? If your experience is anything like our own, your answer will be, "Honestly, a lot of them didn't work out, and a few of them were disasters."

Hiring good people is tough. Let's talk about some steps you can take to minimize the chances that you bring in someone who's a bad fit and maximize the chances that you find someone who can really help you. Here's what we'd suggest:

- Think hard about what this person looks like right now.
- Don't rely on job postings as the primary way to find the person.
- Assume that you'll need to do some selling to convince this person to seriously consider the new job.
- Give the person a couple of performance tests to ensure he can do what you want him to do.

Your ideal candidate is likely already working in a job where she's doing the same sort of work that you'd like her to do for you. Moreover, the person is probably pretty content in that job; she's not looking to make a move. So if she happens to see a job posting you've put on one of the listservs, you can't assume she's automatically going to apply for it. Why would she?

Let's consider some other things that may distinguish this person from other candidates:

- You (or someone on your staff) have seen this person speak at a seminar; you've been impressed by what he had to say and how he expressed his ideas.
- You've read something she's written in a published article or blog post and said to yourself, "This is good. Why aren't we doing this sort of thing?"
- More than one of your colleagues has mentioned this person in passing and said good things about him.
- The person is actively using a stats software package (like SPSS or SAS or Minitab or Data Desk) to do her work. You'd be amazed at how many people we talk to who claim to be doing data mining and predictive modeling but use only Excel.

The policies of your organization may require that you post the job position. From the standpoint of fairness, we agree with such policies. But we don't think posting a job and then looking at only the candidates who apply makes good sense. We've already hinted at why we think so: The person you're looking for probably isn't looking for a new job.

On the other hand, the people who apply are likely to be out of work or dissatisfied with the jobs they're in and ready to make a move. That's fine. You may find one or two excellent candidates in this pool, but we think you'd be better off thinking like an executive recruiter (a "headhunter"). These folks tend to look for a person who is already happy and successful in a job, and they try to lure that person away from his current job.

Be proactive. You have to forage for the person you will eventually hire. We have two suggestions:

- **Use your social and professional network**. If you've worked in the world of fundraising for any amount of time, you know a lot of people who may be able to help you. Start asking them if they know someone who might fit your bill. Call them up. Email them. Before you know it, you'll have a list of people that more than one of the people in your network thinks might be the kind of person you're looking for. Some may know the person well and be able to give you some special insights that you'd never glean from a résumé or an interview.

- **Use the web**. Of course, you'll use the web. Rather than list a comprehensive set of web resources (that may be outdated by the time you read this), we'd suggest you try doing web searches on topics such as "data mining in higher education advancement." You'll find blogs, listservs, and books you've never heard of. Most of all, you'll learn the names of people who do data mining and predictive modeling in our field. Some of them may look like candidates for your job opening. If so, contact them. Perhaps an email saying that you have a job opening that they might be interested in and would it be okay for you to give them a call to "chat" about it. What up-and-coming young professional is not going to respond to an offer like that? And if they don't ... what does that tell you?

You'll need to do some selling. Here's a good chance for you to use a combination of the two skills we think are important in any selling situation: good listening and good talking.

Let's assume you've identified a good candidate. The person hasn't come in for an interview, but you're about to have a phone conversation with her. When you get on the phone, start by briefly explaining why you're calling and why you think the person might be a good match for the job. Don't go on and on. Then give the person a chance to react. For example, this is how the conversation might flow after you've finished your explanation:

Candidate: Well, I'm flattered that you'd call me about this, but I'm pretty happy where I am. It really would take a lot to for me to consider changing jobs, especially right now.

You: (Here is where you need to resist the temptation to start talking about what a great opportunity you're offering. Here's where listening—drawing the person out—is important.) I can understand that. I'd like to hear what it might take to get you to consider making a move.

Candidate: Okay ... hum ... let me think about that for a second.

You: Sure. Take your time. This is important.

Candidate: Well, let's see. I really love what I'm doing, but I'm not wild about the salary I'm making, and I'm not sure whether there is much of a chance for me to move up and take on more responsibility.

You: (Stay in listening mode.) All right, but I bet there are other things that you might want besides a better salary and more of a chance to move up.

Candidate: Well ... this is a little delicate ... I wouldn't want it getting back to the people I work for ...

You: (Here you need to do some reassuring.) They will not hear about any of what you have to tell me. You have my word on that.

Candidate: Okay ... well, the thing is, I'm not sure people above my boss really "get" what I'm doing. I mean, I've shown them how they're wasting huge amounts of money by mailing and calling people who are very unlikely to give, but they still insist on doing things the way we've already done them around here. That's frustrating. That makes me think they don't totally value what I'm trying to do for the school.

To this point you've been a good listener. You've been getting the person to open up about what she likes and doesn't like about her current job and about what some of her career goals are. That's not what most job interviewers do. Sadly, most of them do more of the talking than the person they're interviewing.

But once it's your turn to talk, the important thing is to tie your remarks into what you've heard from the candidate. In this example, you'd obviously want to address salary, opportunity for growth, and the impact the candidate's work would have on the way your institution raises money. You can throw in things about how beautiful your campus is, your excitement about the new campaign, etc. But don't do that at the expense of talking candidly about the things that are of concern to the candidate.

If you've done your job well, your target candidate may have already talked himself into being interested in working for you. But there's still a lot you don't know about this person. Hiring always entails some risk. You never really know if the person is going to work out until after he's been on the job awhile. To help reduce the risk, we'd recommend that you give any of your serious candidates two performance tests:

1. Building a mini model with real data you can provide from your prospective donor/donor database
2. Explaining the results of the model to you and other people who might be working with the candidate.

Before we explain the performance tests, we should say that how the candidate responds to your asking may give you some important information about what he'll be like when he actually comes to work for you. A positive, enthusiastic response ("Oh, I'd love to do that!") is obviously what you want to hear. A hesitant, ho-hum response is not what you want to hear. If he says something like "I'm really busy right now. How soon do you need it?" when he's supposedly trying to impress you, imagine how he'll respond to requests when he's landed the job.

You will ask the candidate to build a simple model. We'll assume that you work for a higher education institution, but you should be able to do something similar if you work for a general nonprofit. Here are some details:

1. Prepare an Excel file with the following fields for either your entire solicitable alumni database, or a random sample of at least 10,000 records from that database that includes the following fields:
   - Unique ID number (be sure this is the only identifying information you include in the file. No names, telephone numbers, email addresses. Nothing that anyone could use to reach out to these folks.)
   - Total amount lifetime giving
   - Home phone present (Yes/No)
   - Business phone present (Yes/No)
   - Email address present (Yes/No)
   - Marital status field (include all codes)
   - Preferred year of graduation
   - Events attended after graduation (Yes/No)

2. Send the candidate the file asking her to build a predictive model of some kind using these data. She can do that however she wants to, but you'd like her to come up with a score for each record in the file that can be used to save money and generate more revenue on appeals.
3. Ask her to prepare a presentation for you and your staff of the results of the model and how it could be used. You should say the candidate can do the presentation either on a conference call using the web or when she comes in for the interview.

The candidate's presentation will tell you a lot about whether or not you've found the right person. When the presentation is over, you should able to say "I strongly agree" to the following three statements:

1. You understood what the person was telling you and showing you. That is, you were more enlightened than you were confused.
2. The candidate made a compelling case for how your internal data (like what you provided) could be used to do a more efficient job of raising money at your institution. That is, you were inspired and excited by what you heard and saw.
3. The candidate answered questions that you and your team posed in a clear, helpful, and noncondescending manner.

If you don't strongly agree with those statements, you probably need to keep looking.

Working with Vendors

We believe in the value of nonprofits learning how to mine their own data. Beyond the surface similarities in the organization of institutional data, any individual database is a complex organism that can take years to get to know deeply. No one outside your organization to whom you've handed a flat file for analysis is going to understand that complexity and explore it to full advantage like someone who works with it every day. And no external data source will be as powerfully predictive of giving to your cause as the history of interactions with your constituents you have recorded in your own database. As well, outsourced analytics work tends to be project-oriented: When the product is delivered, the relationship is over, precisely when the work of evaluating results really should begin so that improvements can be developed as the cycle continues. Embedding analytics in the organizational culture is difficult to accomplish when conducted as a series of discrete projects.

That said, at some time or another you will encounter firms that offer analytics services that include wealth screenings and developing custom predictive models. What about them? It may make sense to outsource the work when it isn't possible to develop the talent in-house. Or maybe in-house model-building is possible but still a long way off; analytics will pay off right now, so why not pay someone else to do it? A vendor might also have a wider range of approaches and techniques to draw on than an in-house practitioner has, and therefore more likely to have the appropriate solution. (Of course, that depends on the vendor.) A vendor might also have better access to external data sources, particularly related to individual wealth, or philanthropic activity outside your organization.

Just remember: Learning as much as you can will be a big help when it comes time to negotiate with vendors and, eventually, work with your chosen vendor in a fruitful partnership. Skills development is not *necessarily* about replacing outside services; it can also be about helping us to be more knowledgeable purchasers. The client is in control of choosing or rejecting a vendor: Any knowledge acquired will be an asset in making good choices.

At the very least, some analytics knowledge will make it less likely you'll be taken in by promises that can't be delivered on. For example, predictive modeling cannot yield a list of guaranteed major gift donors: Predictive modeling does not pick sure winners, it only identifies subpopulations of your constituency with elevated probabilities of doing whatever it is you're hoping for, including stepping up to make a major gift. Vendors who talk this game are telling you they can pick winning lotto numbers; it's best to avoid them.

In picking the right vendor to work with, consider whether you are getting value beyond your short-term needs. A number of analytics vendors have well-deserved reputations for being educational leaders in the field. They're the ones who share their methods freely, who help clients understand what they're getting and how it ought to be used, and who empower their clients to work with their own data. It's not hard to figure out who those vendors are: They're the ones giving webinars, presenting at conferences, writing for blogs, and sharing in various other ways that go beyond simply advertising their presence in the market. Just look on the Internet. On the other hand, there are vendors who are not willing to explain their methods—your data goes into their black box, and out pops a set of scores, as if by magic. Vendors who won't or can't explain their wizardry are best avoided.

The benefits of having a little analytics knowledge accrue at every stage of the vendor-customer relationship, for both parties:

- Knowledgeable purchasers are more likely to know what questions to ask of prospective vendors, and they will make better purchasing decisions. Vendors will have already seen many similar scenarios and can certainly help with envisioning solutions, but it would be better if end-users already had some concept of what the solution should look like.

- Organizations that can translate their needs and priorities into specific goals to communicate to a vendor are more likely to work well with that vendor, particularly during the sometimes challenging data collection and preparation phase of the project.

- After the purchase, the product is more likely to be deployed properly, or the service more likely to be well-used and evaluated, if staff have some understanding of analytics and what the purchase is designed to accomplish.

- And finally, as a natural consequence of the previous three points, knowledgeable buyers are more likely to be pleased with what they've bought. This increases the likelihood that buyer and vendor will enjoy a working relationship that extends into the future, beyond the one-time purchase.

Perhaps you work for an organization that has always outsourced its analytics work. Is there a problem with that? Perhaps not. But that's not a good enough reason to stay in the dark about your data. And we remain convinced that it makes no sense to spend a lot of money on external data before you've mined the vast potential in the internal, affinity-related data you already have.

part **2**

YOUR DATA-DRIVEN JOB

Numbers, Analysis, and
So Much More

IN PART 1 WE OBSERVED that in our experience, adoption of data-driven methods often gets its start via the initiative and interest of an employee or employees in an organization, rather than from that organization's leadership. But without support and vision from people in charge, analytics will not take hold and become part of the culture. So in the first part of this book we've tried to come at it from every angle that might concern a director or vice president.

This part of the book swings around to look at the subject from the point of view of the person who's actually doing the work, or aspires to do the work, of data analysis. Where up to now we've talked about orienting the organization, now we will address the individual employee and his or her skills. We'll start with the "soft skills" essential to becoming an analyst, and then some of the hard skills that make up the foundation of analytical work. After that, we'll describe what we mean when we talk about "analysis," which will lead into showing you analyses that we've conducted using the type of data you're already familiar with: alumni and donor data.

If you're not interested in some extra work and responsibility in your job, then perhaps data work is not for you—because the person in an enlightened organization who understands data at that level is going to be present at the table where decisions are made. And if your presence is *not* welcomed at the table, because the organization is not that enlightened, then another workplace might be in your future. Either way, if your goal is to become an analyst, or at least incorporate analysis in your work, you should not expect to remain behind the scenes in a minor supporting role for the rest of your career. You'll be too valuable for that.

chapter 3

Soft Skills

hen you pick up a book about data mining and predictive modeling, you expect the authors to cover a lot of technical stuff. And there's some technical stuff in this book. On the other hand, any data mining and modeling you do in the world of advancement involves working with people. From our own trips, stumbles, and occasional leaps forward, we can assure you of this: The social skills you bring to the table when you work with people can make a huge difference in either helping your institution embrace data-driven decision-making, or letting them give it a polite wave as they trot along doing what they've always done to raise money or deal with alumni.

Before we jump into what some of these important skills are, we need to be clear that we don't expect anyone to get a personality transplant. Let's use ourselves as examples. One personality trait often mentioned in connection with data analysts, researchers, or others who work in supporting roles is introversion. It's a stereotype, and one that often doesn't hold.

Kevin

I'm more of an introvert than an extrovert. What does that mean? I think it means that, although I am not a loner, I find that talking—especially talking to groups—drains me of energy. I could not imagine a workday without my colleagues around to consult with, and I've learned to enjoy giving presentations to audiences at work and at conferences. But in the search for balance in life, I keep guard over my quiet time. That's when I write, and it's also when I am most creative and productive in my work with data. Like anyone else I need contact with other people, but that part tends to take care of itself.

Peter

I'm more of an extrovert than an introvert. What does that mean? I think it means that I get a lot of energy from people, even though I often need a break from them. But I'm never going to stop trying to talk to folks on the street, in coffee shops, gas stations, wherever. It's just too much fun. You make me stop doing that, I'm going to shrivel up and blow away.

I've got a bit of a temper. Got that from my dad. I've gotten better at controlling my temper as the decades have rolled by, but it's still my constant companion. If I'm driving along on an interstate and some clown gets on my tail, I immediately get bent out of shape. I want to throw some coffee out my window that will splatter his windshield. I don't do that. (Linda has threatened to leave me if I ever do.) I hit the windshield wash that sends a light mist on the other guy's windshield. Unless the guy's a real jerk, he usually backs up a bit. But in my heart of hearts, I still want to do the coffee thing.

None of us is going to change the essential person we are. So when we talk about skills, we are talking about qualities that anyone can develop, not fixed aspects of personality. Are some personality types better suited to working with data? Perhaps. Good analysts are both creative and methodical, for example. While it may be possible for a person to become more creative or methodical, those qualities are too broad to deal with in this book. That said, we do believe there are some general abilities we can develop to make us more effective consultants to the people whose problems we are trying to help solve. Here are three:

- Listening
- Communicating
- Growing

Listening

This may be the most important skill of all, so let's begin with it. Listening and communicating are related, of course, but listening is so important that it deserves to be treated separately. By "listening" we mean *active* listening. True listening is not a passive activity. It's aimed at extracting meaning from what is spoken by another person, sometimes another person who may not be able to articulate what it is they want. It involves carefully evaluating what a person is saying in the moment and asking follow-up questions to clarify what he means. This is the kind of listening a journalist employs during an interview with a subject who may be reluctant or unable to make a clear statement of what he or she thinks, a situation that calls for some skillful prodding by the interviewer. In our context, a director or other decision-maker may have difficulty stating a business problem in such a way as to make it addressable by analytics.

The business problem may initially be stated as, "We need to increase the number of donors to the annual fund"; but that's only the surface of the problem, not enough to build a model on. The listener should recognize that key information is missing, and ask questions: Do you mean acquiring new donors? Or should we identify lapsed donors who are most likely to be reactivated? Do you intend to boost donor numbers primarily by a phone campaign, or mail, or online? The answers to these questions may lead to a variety of definitions of the real business problem, which will suggest the most appropriate model or models to build. For example, perhaps what is needed is a pool of young-alumni prospects who have high propensity to give as well as high propensity to be receptive to email solicitation. This is not a formulation that a director of the annual fund is likely to come up with on her own. It is a product of a two-way conversation that entails a lot of active listening.

Sometimes the data miner is also the end-user. Prospect researchers who build predictive models may use their scores to prioritize assignment of new prospects to gift officers, for example, and no one else sees those scores. In that case, the conversation about the business problem is an internal one, taking place inside the head of a single person, and the conversion of business problem to model definition is hidden from view. In an organization seeking to employ analytics across all operations, however, the analyst and the end-user are going to be different people with potentially divergent points of view and different ways of expressing their thoughts. Again, far from being a passive state, listening involves not just questioning, but translating as well.

Why *translating*? Because the analyst works in the zone between two types of understanding: the business understanding, using the language of fundraisers and alumni officers, and the data understanding, the language of IT or information systems. New data miners and analysts may come from either field, the business side or the technical side, but they need to learn the language employed by their colleagues on the other side. The analyst herself uses a third language, the statistical language of her craft, so it's a bit like the United Nations! Let's not exaggerate: Learning to navigate through these differences is not nearly as complex as learning to speak a true language, nor is mastery a requirement in order to do useful work. But conceptually it's helpful to think of the job as being like that of a translator.

All of this assumes that you're working with people who already understand that you're going to use your skills to help them. Listening is also an important skill to cultivate if you are at an even earlier stage: trying to convince people that a predictive model will be of use to them. You will need to understand what it is that person most needs—a question that will change depending on circumstances. When advocating for data-driven decision-making, you will have much better luck if your innovations are a response to current need than if they are just "cool ideas" that you'd like other people to get on board with.

Don't get us wrong, we are big fans of "just cool"; a neat idea might be the answer to a good question that has yet to be asked. But in any environment that is bound by tradition and unfriendly to innovation for its own sake (and fundraising would be such an environment), listening to the fears and hopes of your co-workers will provide focus to your work. Those fears and hopes might be documented in an annual plan, which you should be familiar with. But first and foremost, you must be a listener.

At staff meetings, in presentations, over lunch: Keep your ear to the ground. Think of the planned giving officer who has thousands of alumni over the age of 55 who all have giving patterns that she thinks suggest good potential for a bequest—where does she begin? Think of the annual giving staffer who has enough room in the budget to mail only one-fifth of his prospective donor pool for acquisition—how does he narrow the field and maximize dollars? Or the prospect researcher in major gifts—her office has spent tens of thousands of dollars on a wealth screening, but she is beginning to realize that she doesn't know how to gauge affinity. You can help all of these people. What you do will be useful *and* exceedingly cool.

Communicating

Often the success or failure of your work depends on end users. If they don't use your model scores, for example, then there wasn't much point in producing them in the first place. If you've listened carefully, and you've done your best to address their needs head-on, you have a better chance that users will have some faith in your methods.

You're not home free, though: Building models requires consultation at the level of defining the problem or target, but after that, consulting with end-users may provide no additional benefit. Once you have defined the problem, you will find the answer in the data, not via more consultation. The best predictors of giving, for example, will be revealed in the analysis, not in any guidance from domain experts such as fundraisers. They may offer excellent suggestions that lead to the discovery of predictors you were not aware of, but at this stage in the process their experience and intuition take a back seat. Your analysis might confirm their observations and biases, but it is just as likely to turn up surprises, non-intuitive insights, or findings that directly contradict what they have long believed. That is the nature of data mining. If its only purpose were to confirm our gut instincts, it wouldn't be nearly as useful. The disruptive nature of the work, unfortunately, may cause difficulties when it's time for end-users to accept what you have found.

You need to become comfortable with "selling," with explaining your ideas and presenting your findings in a compelling way that does not confuse or bore. If you were able to show your fundraising colleagues that high-scoring segments of the alumni population give a lot more than the others and that low-scoring segments give little or nothing, you'd think your work was done. Alas, no. Don't assume that you'll simply be able to hand off the data, because if data mining is not yet part of your institution's culture, it's more than likely your findings will be under-used.

Ensure that your end-users know what to do with their scores. Be prepared to make suggestions for applications. At the other end, you'll need to understand how your colleagues implemented their scores in order to do any follow-up analysis of the effectiveness of your model. For example, if you plan to analyze the results of the annual fund telephone campaign, you'll need to know exactly who was called and who wasn't, before you can compare scores against giving.

End-users of analytics are only one of the parties you'll need to communicate with. You'll also need to talk to upper management to get their support, and you'll need to work with advancement services or your IT person on some of the technical details of acquiring and understanding data. Working with these two groups of people involves presenting and explaining your ideas clearly.

Selling your work to end-users is only part of the job. You won't succeed on your own in having your work integrated into your department's operations if you don't have the support of leadership. You have to sell up as well. It is increasingly the case that vice presidents and directors are hearing about data-driven decision-making from all sides already, but it's your job to connect that abstract idea with your ability to make it real for the organization, and you need to win their support to make it happen.

There are right ways and wrong ways to sell, however.

Kevin

I used to follow a great blog called 43folders.com, created by Merlin Mann. His boss and friend said to him one day, "Y'know, Merlin, we're really satisfied with the actual work you do, but is there any way you could do it without showing so much ... I don't know ... mental sausage?"

Data mining and predictive modeling and cool data stuff are all exercises in discovery. When we discover something new, our natural urge is to share. In the past, I tended to share the wrong way: carefully revealing my discovery as if the process were unfolding in real time. These expositions (usually in the form of a Word document emailed around) would usually be rather long. The central message would often be buried in detail which someone not inhabiting my head would regard as extraneous.

Don't expect people to follow your plot: They're too busy. You need to make your point quickly and clearly. Learn to use the charting options available in Excel or some other software to explain it visually. Offer to explain it face-to-face. Offer to present on it. And don't assume that anyone understands.

From the first step, to the end, and around the cycle again, you will need to shepherd your work along, explaining things in language your audience will understand.

Growing

The analyst "type," if there is such a thing, is also distinguished by an avid curiosity about the subject of his work, and an orientation toward personal growth.

Even in this time of rapidly growing awareness of the power of data analysis and the popularity of buzz terms such as *big data,* it is very likely that these concepts represent new approaches that have not been tried at your organization before. As a consequence, the required skills and approaches are not part of anyone's current job description. In other words, bringing your organization into the age of data implies a redefinition of the work you do. You will enjoy greater success if you think in terms of personal growth.

Contributing to the creation of a new position can be a fun and creative process, but it requires your active engagement. Don't count on your boss or employer to "get it," absolving you of any need to push the agenda. Even among upper management who will say they "get it," there is a lot of lip service paid to the idea of data-driven decision-making. They hear the buzz everywhere they go, and no one wants to admit they aren't innovating.

So as a staff member, it may be up to you to carry the flag. Presumably you're already quite busy at work, and there is little time and few resources available for extra projects. You will either have to make time at work, or make an investment of your own personal time.

Your own time? Before you say "That's too much to ask," consider how much of your life you spend at work. It IS your life. None of us has so much of life that we can afford to just put in the time at the office, and hope to do all our "real" living outside of work. Now consider how much of your work is not congruent with your talents and interests. Is there not some small step you could take on your own time to move in a different direction? Maybe you can get a little better at doing your job, to become more engaged. Or maybe you can redefine the job itself. Or it might be time to move on. In any case, don't you owe it to yourself to do something?

We all know people who have a very passive attitude about work, people who believe their professional development is their employers' responsibility. These are the people who would never pay to attend a workshop that wasn't covered by their employer, regardless of how helpful it would be in their future career. They would never buy a book like this one on their own dime. They would complain that they never get to go to a conference—yet they have never put together a proposal to sell their employer on the idea, outlining which sessions they want to attend and how it will address their employer's needs while enhancing their own growth.

Some night soon, turn off the television and spend some of your own time getting your ideas down about why your employer ought to send you to a conference. And it probably wouldn't kill you to crack a work-related book over the weekend. You don't need to be sitting in a cubicle to play with data, either. Work-life balance is all well and good—until the half of your life that you call "work" is no longer fulfilling or helping you to grow. Then it's time to recognize that work and life are part of a whole, and none of it should ever consist of just putting in time.

Just leaving your job or angling for promotions are not solutions in themselves; there are people who change their environments regularly and never find happiness. It's about being happy where you are. You may need to change your environment, but more likely you will need to make investments in yourself.

Many of us who work in higher education advancement might immediately think of earning another degree. Our investment need not be as structured, directed, and demanding as a new degree, however. It may simply be allowing time for play. If there's one element that is the mark of a successful analyst, it's a sense of play. Again and again we hear people say that they feel a little guilty setting aside the urgent task (invariably unimportant in the long run) to conduct some sort of experiment or analysis with data. They're the ones who will be successful in this field. An idle thought or a stray idea will somehow grow, connect with other stray bits, and solidify into something useful: A new way of doing things, or a whole new thing to be doing. Whether it's creating a new process at work or changing the path of your life, the process is the same. The grit in the oyster around which the pearl formed was initially nothing more than an interesting distraction ... while the top priorities of just a year ago have mysteriously vaporized, leaving nothing of substance behind.

Not every vague idea finds application. Maybe most won't. The point is this: Your basket of vague ideas comes first. The problems, needs, applications will follow someday. The next action is to create some way to capture your stray thoughts and ideas. Could be scraps of paper in a folder, a notebook, a free app such as Evernote—whatever. Something you can review periodically, in order to connect today's mental noodling with tomorrow's real needs. Then, when there is time free for playing with those ideas, seize it. Whether that is work time or personal time doesn't much matter.

chapter 4

Hard Skills

nalytics can be a highly technical field, but analysts work at all levels of technical proficiency. There may be no minimum level of expertise required before you can begin to provide key insights for your organization. Yes, it's true that you should be comfortable using a computer, and you will eventually need to learn the rudiments of a statistical software package and come to know your way around your institution's data. These are not insurmountable barriers to anyone with sufficient interest. In this field, understanding your organization and its goals (called "domain knowledge") comes before technical know-how. So don't worry, you may be more ready to learn than you think. In any case, you should be aware that true experts are quite rare. No one knows it all—there will always be more to learn!

We would be lying if we did not admit that on the road to learning analytical skills, there is a series of barriers. For example:

- Many of the relevant books and online resources are couched in the language of statistics. Which elements of statistics are necessary to understand and which are optional is not made explicit. As well, there are numerous approaches to modeling, which confuses anyone trying to focus on the approach that works best for his particular application.

- As well, the mechanics of modeling—the specific steps to follow—differ from software package to software package. A development office staff person looking for the exact set of instructions to conduct one specific task is not likely to find what she's looking for.

- Finally, the would-be analyst needs to work with data from his own database and learn how to look at it in a whole new way. It helps if the teaching resource you're using talks about data from an alumni or fundraising perspective, but even within that world, everyone's data is different.

Any one of these three barriers may be tough to surmount on its own; but the fact that all three occur together can stop people in their tracks. It's like someone who's never been in a kitchen before needing to cook a specific meal for which there is no recipe—because in the analytics kitchen, a recipe is not only specific to the desired dish (the outcome), but to the oven (software) and to the ingredients on hand (data). Any specific recipe would have to be adapted, which is too much to ask of the beginner cook. Conversely, any overall method that attempts to explain more than one dish, more than one brand of oven, and an endless variety of ingredients is too general to be called a recipe.

For these reasons, when people ask how to get started in predictive modeling, we encourage them to seek one-on-one training. Conference sessions can inspire you and lead to a lot of great ideas and new contacts to turn to for help, but without continuing guidance it's easy to lose your way in the forest of details. Books are great, but there isn't a single book that contains a step-by-step guide that covers more than a fraction of fundraising modeling situations. The Internet can be a wonderful resource, but much of what you'll find is highly technical, doesn't apply directly to our purposes, and is completely lacking a road map for the uninitiated.

So here's a different approach. In the sections that follow, you will find suggestions for moving in the right direction by developing a general set of skills that will begin to lay the foundations for doing analytical work. As you progress, you will start thinking about data in a new way, and we hope you'll be empowered to reproduce some of the studies in this book using your own data—to learn to do by doing.

Seven Building Blocks for Data Work

Whether you're interested in predictive modeling or you just want to become more data-oriented in your work, here are seven steps to get you started on your journey. Along the way you will acquire skills that will prove useful again and again. None of these steps involves using stats software. Some of them involve Excel, the software you're most likely to already have on your desktop.

1. Get access
Arrange to get direct access to some of the key tables of your organization's database. If data entry is part of your job, you may already have "write" access, but

ideally you will want to have "query" access. In any event, get as much access as allowable. Just knowing which tables contain what types of data will prove valuable in the future. If you can't get your hands on either the database or a reporting tool that queries the database, skip to Number 3.

2. Get data

Learn how to build a simple query to extract data on your own. Most of us who work at institutions with complex databases rely on our technical people to pull the data we need. Unfortunately, submitting requests to someone else for data, having to define exactly what it is you want, and then waiting for the request to be fulfilled—all of that is death to creative data exploration. By the time you've gone back and forth a few times with the person in advancement services who's trying to figure out what you want, you've lost the initial impulse to explore that spurred you on in the first place. Learning to query the database might seem like a pain initially, but the flexibility this affords you to grab the data you need at any time will be extremely valuable when you later get into more data-focused work. Of all the building blocks, this one will take the longest; but you don't need to become proficient, you just need to get started.

3. Get functional

Once you've pulled some data, or have had it pulled for you, nine times out of 10 you're going to be working with it in Excel. You will need a stats package for serious data work, but Excel has its uses as well. You should learn how to use some very basic spreadsheet formulas. If you have a file open with some columns of data in it, click into any cell in the first blank column to the right of your data, and type "=". This lets Excel know that you want to write a formula. Formulas usually perform some operation on data that's sitting in another cell, whether it's manipulating a text string or performing a numerical calculation. If you already know a few formulas, go a little further by exploring conditional ("IF") statements and nested formulas (formulas within formulas). We can't get into specifics here, but just play with the program's Formulas menu options, and look for how-to's online; searching the Internet for tutorials is frequently better than relying on Excel's help file. The structure and logic of formulas is something you will encounter again and again, not just in Excel but in query-building and in handling data with other software packages. People are intimidated by formulas because they can appear complex, but just take it slow, learning new formulas as you need them.

4. Get savvy

Acquire or brush up on some (very) basic knowledge of stats terms. Start with learning the meaning, proper usage, and calculation of percentages, means (averages), and medians. A lot of the work of looking for patterns in data involves nothing more than comparing percentages, averages, and medians between two or more groups. If these concepts are old hat, find definitions for other terms you will encounter, including *quartile, decile, percentile, correlation, distribution,* and any other unfamiliar statistical term you come across. (The concept of correlation is especially key in data mining.) When you search these terms, look for articles that explain them in a way that makes sense to you. If the discussion starts getting too technical, back out of it and follow another search result. There are dozens of ways to explain these concepts, and someone out there has expressed it in language you will understand.

5. Get charts
Go back to Excel, and learn how to make bar charts, which in Excel are called "column" charts. The best way to explore data is to display it visually. It's also the best way to communicate your findings to others. There are plenty of sexy ways to display data visually, but most of our data stories are best told with simple bar charts. Learn the various types of bar charts (simple, stacked, 100% stacked). When you get proficient with making bar charts, try converting them to line plots. Ask yourself, Which types of data lend themselves to bars and which to lines?

6. Get visual
Learn how to lay out a slide in PowerPoint or Keynote. Yes, we all dislike sitting through slide presentations. So don't make the same mistakes other people do. Fill your screen with a visual display of data instead of text—copy and paste your bar chart onto a blank slide. Resize the chart and adjust labels as needed to ensure maximum visibility. Now instead of reading text from a slide, you can talk about the picture. In the previous chapter we said that sharing and explaining your work with others is a key part of promoting data-driven decision-making in your organization. Being able to convey your point visually will be a big step in the right direction.

7. Get it down
Acquire the habit of documenting your work. This serves a number of purposes. First, your notes are a placeholder for your explorations. Seeking insights with data takes time, so keeping notes will let you know from day to day where you left off. Recording what you've learned already about your data means you don't have to keep re-learning the same things every time you begin a related project. Second, if you want to share your discoveries with others, it's a lot easier to pause every once in a while during your work to take a few notes and capture a chart or two than it is to write a discussion paper from scratch after the fact. Third, your documentation is an important record for others to build on your work.

These skills will prove invaluable for any future work involving data, because they underlie the general steps that many real analyses tend to follow:

1. Formulate a question you would like an answer to.
2. Find out where the answer is likely to reside (database tables).
3. Isolate the data you need to study (query the database).
4. Manipulate and clean the data to make it suitable for analysis (which may involve Excel or other software).
5. Apply the analytical tools that might help answer the question (compare two or more groups statistically).
6. Visualize the data (charts).
7. Document and share your findings (via a presentation or discussion paper).

In a way, listing a set of required skills to learn is putting the cart before the horse. Having an interesting question or problem to focus on, and the curiosity to embark on finding answers, is enough to pull that cart in the right direction. Just jump on for the ride, and you'll pick up the skills you need as you go along.

The Education of a Data Analyst

We get a lot of questions from people interested in not only enhancing their job skills, but in taking their career to a whole other place, via analytics. Questions such as: What do I have to study? How long will it take? Can someone my age get hired in this field?

We have different takes on this question. Let's let Peter go first.

Here's the assumption I'm making about you: You're interested in a career change that would have you spending the lion's share of your professional time on data mining and predictive modeling in the general arena of fundraising and advancement. You'd be doing this work as an employee of an institution, or as a consultant, or as some combination of the two.

Then the question becomes "What will I need to get from here to there?" The answer is: a considerable helping of passion. Why? Too many roadblocks. Call it people, call it society, call it Western culture, call it the nature of our existence here on this planet. If you try to do something that you really love full-time (especially if you want somebody to pay you to do it), you will run into all sorts of obstacles that seem designed to discourage you and derail you. Think about anyone who's wanted to become an actor, a professional athlete, a physician, a published novelist ... every one of them will tell you stories of frustration, despair, outrage, and humiliation before they got what they wanted, or they finally threw in the towel, declaring: "Ain't worth the pain."

I wish it were easier for people to achieve their professional dreams. On the other hand (my curmudgeon-like nature notwithstanding), I am an optimist at my core. I believe that, if you want something badly enough, you can get it, or you can come so close to getting it that you end up saying, "Yep, I'm doing something I really love. I'm there."

So what should I say next to really help you? I decided to tell you how I got to where I am now, doing something I truly love. It's a story that goes back almost 45 years as of this writing.

Fall of 1967 through spring of 1968

I was back in college, after a two-year hiatus, to finish up my final year. (I had been thrown out in 1965 for reasons I won't bore you with.) I was taking a course in introductory statistics taught by a psych professor. The guy was boring, uninspiring, and inaccessible. The text we were using was abysmally written. Nonetheless, I became aware that I liked statistics in a way that I had not liked algebra, geometry, and the two-semester required course in calculus I had taken as a freshman. I started fantasizing about analyzing data from experiments that I could then write up as journal articles. I began to consider going to graduate school for more advanced training in psychology, where I could get seriously involved in research.

That's where I remember encountering the first obstacle. None, not one, of my psych professors was encouraging when I brought up the idea of going to grad school. "Your grades prior to coming back here to finish up aren't going to help." "We think you can do the work in grad school, but they're gonna be interested in people who have more to offer than you do."

I still think back on that and imagine all the things I would say to those guys if I were to run into them today. (And people wonder why I don't give the school a penny.) It was a setback, but I couldn't chase the thoughts of data analysis from my head.

Summer of 1968 to fall of 1969

With no help from the professors, I landed a job at something called LIAMA just before I left school, diploma finally in hand. It was a not-for-profit organization whose mission was to do, among other things, behavioral research for the life insurance industry.

I was only there for 15 months, but what a breath of fresh air that place was. How so?

- They had guys with doctorates in the behavioral sciences with whom I could sit and talk about statistics and research methodology. For the most part, they were friendly and supportive of my ideas, crudely formed as they were.

- I had access to a computer that allowed me to learn firsthand about correlation analysis, multiple regression, and factor analysis. I remember submitting a "job" (consisting of hundreds of punch cards) to the computer center in the morning, going to lunch, and champing at the bit to see what awaited me upon my return to the office. Often it was an aborted attempt that meant going back through the cards to find some tiny error and start the process all over again. Didn't matter. I was in hog heaven. I had a 90-minute round-trip commute in a little VW that put my life at risk five days a week. Most of that time I spent thinking about data stuff and what I was going to do next with that big old blunderbuss of a computer.

- All the guys with doctorates were supportive of my going on to grad school and wrote me strong recommendations to help me get in.

Fall of 1969 to fall of 1973

In September off I went to Teachers College in New York City. It was right across 121st Street from the Ivy League school that had spawned it but treated it like the child of a mistress it didn't want the world to know about. Fine by me. I'd had more than enough of insufferable elitism.

TC is a big old rambling place that is a mix of the 19th, 20th, and 21st centuries. That doesn't set it apart from lots of universities. What does set it apart is that it is all encased in a big city block. And I think every day I walked into that place I felt as if I was stepping into a museum with the ghosts of John Dewey and E. L. Thorndike ambling alongside me down some of its high-ceilinged halls.

Among all the important things that happened to me during those four years, some I call "brakes" and others I call "accelerators" in my quest to become a professional data analyst.

Let's do the brakes first.

Fellow students. Most of my friends throughout my life have been outgoing types who get a lot of energy from people. That was certainly the case at TC. These folks were there to get their academic tickets punched so they could go out into the world as therapists and help struggling souls with their neuroses. They were smart and quite capable of handling the required stats and methods courses, but they did not like them. They would listen patiently to some of my ideas on data analysis, but they simply would not engage me. They also sent the subtle message that stats and methods weren't of much use in solving the pressing human problems of the day—like civil rights or a psychotic president who had us quagmired in a war in Southeast Asia.

Stodgy professors. The faculty at TC who were experts in the quantitative side of things didn't have the greatest social skills. Two of them were insufferably arrogant, and I gave them a wide berth. The rest were nice enough, but they were just too nerdy to sit down and chew the fat with. (I'll tell you about the one exception a little later.)

My major adviser. This guy was a live wire. He oozed energy and enthusiasm, and he was loaded down with ideas on how to cure society's ills. He roped me in. He offered me work that had to do with his ideas, and I needed that work. I was poor as a church mouse. He also came up with an idea for a dissertation that I could get rolling on right away. Things were looking pretty good. But as time passed it became clearer and clearer to me that this guy was not focused. Every time I'd try to move things forward on the dissertation path, he would go off on a tangent. After two years of that, I declared to myself, "Enough! I have to pick another topic, one that he won't know a thing about so he'll stop getting in my way."

Archaic technology. Most of you who are reading this will have only heard of the days of punch cards and massive computers. I wrote my dissertation (and a book a few years later) on a typewriter! If back then the technology of today had been available, I would not have spent two decades doing something I really didn't like.

Now let's talk about the accelerators.

A vast library. With the coming of the Internet and now all the cool ways to access it, libraries aren't places that graduate students physically spend a lot of time in. (At least, I don't think so.) In the early '70s, of course, that was not the case. If you had to do research, you went to the library. And TC had a great one. Just the smell of the place would pull me in to browse among the thousands and thousands of square feet (spread out over three floors) devoted to books and journals and completed dissertations, many of which had to do with the quantitative topics I was interested in. I particularly remember being on the lookout for new editions of *Educational and Psychological Measurement*, *Psychomerika*, *Psychological Bulletin*, and other journals that dealt (and still do) with stats and methodology. Yep, I was a geek on steroids.

Tutoring/Consulting. As fellow students learned of my interest in stats and the fact that it came easily to me, I began to get questions about whether or not I offered thesis/dissertation services. My typical response was, "No, but tell me what you're struggling with. Maybe I can help." In spite of their insistence, I could not bring myself to ask these folks for money. I had a good paying job at the university, and the problems they put in my lap were compensation enough. But I do remember one lady whom I helped (she was old enough to have been my mom) shoving three crisp $50 bills into my hand just before Christmas. "Buy your wife a nice present, dear," she said.

My dissertation. "Effects of Coarse Grouping and Skewed Marginal Distributions on the Pearson Product-Moment Correlation Coefficient." I don't know about you, but I think that title is catchy. Except for the punch cards, I had a ball with this project. I purposely picked the two toughest methodological professors at TC to be on my committee. When I finally got the darn thing done, my orals were a breeze. And my erstwhile major adviser who sat in on them? He didn't dare ask one question because he had no idea what it was about. Yowsah!

Dick Lindeman. Dick was a Korean War veteran who had grown up in Wisconsin. What he was doing in Manhattan always puzzled me. He just didn't fit in. But he was great to me, and I took every stats course he taught and got him to head up my dissertation committee. I remember his saying to me, "You should always be asking us (meaning my committee members) whether what you've done so far is enough to have us approve it." I chuckled and said, "Come on, Dr. Lindeman, you're not supposed to tell me that. You're supposed to keep telling me I haven't yet done enough." He smirked and said, "Just telling you what my committee told me when I got my degree." Gotta love a guy like that.

1973–1977

From the standpoint of data analysis, the only really good thing about this period for me was meeting and marrying my wife, Linda. She was then and remains totally supportive of my love for data analysis. Professionally it was a dud. I had two crappy jobs during this time working for two guys who had doctorates in psychology and they, in spite of very different personalities, were lousy bosses. Not bad guys, just ... just not inspiring.

I did do some stats tutoring during this time (now for remuneration). Good stuff. But it was nowhere enough to compensate for the day jobs. Toward the end of 1977 I had had enough of working for someone else. On October 1, I was on my own as a consultant and have not held a real job since. And, man, was that ever the right decision!

1977–1996

When this period began, I was 34. When it ended I was 52. During that 18-year stretch I did very little data stuff. I was working with an old friend from graduate school doing small business counseling, making some pretty good money, but not liking it all that much.

But there was a bright spot. It was the fall of 1993 and I was looking at a magazine for Apple users in a sleazy store that sold videotapes and ... you don't wanna know. The magazine says there's this really cool stats software package for Macs called Data Desk. The next day I call the 800 number and who should answer? None other than John Sammis. He cuts me a deal and sends me the package and I start using it right away on my Mac.

That was a pivotal event. All of a sudden I had a tool that could do things that were not even a fantasy when I left TC in 1973. I was blown away; I realized how much I wanted to get back to doing analytic work. It was the beginning of the end for my old career, and the beginning of the beginning for my new one.

The next three years were not easy.

I came face to face with how much I didn't like the consulting work I was doing. It's painful to dredge this up, but I'll sum it up this way. I was working with someone whom I never should have been working with in the first place. (We'll leave it at that.) Worse, I didn't like the clients we were working with. For the most part, they were small-business owners who weren't nice to the employees who worked for them, and they weren't receptive to the feedback they were paying us to give them. But most of all, I had to own up to the fact that I was not temperamentally suited for the work. If you're primary inclination is to tell your clients you think they are narcissistic jerks, it's time to find another way to make a living.

I didn't know where I was going to find analytics work that would be fulfilling. In those days, the Internet was just sort of an idea, not the awesome resource it is today. So I floundered around looking for possibilities. The one place where I got some traction was a small firm that badly needed the kind of help I offered, but the owner was a challenging character. He gave me an entrée into the world I wanted to be in, and I owe him a debt of gratitude for that. But I just couldn't stand the guy.

1996–1999

Three things happened during this period that firmly launched me into the field of data mining and predictive modeling for fundraising:

I met Bo Schnurr. Bo is a genius and a bit eccentric, as most geniuses are. One day in October of 1997 he mentioned the term *list scoring*. The conversation then went sort of like this:

Peter: What's that?

Bo: Well, all fundraising institutions now have electronic lists of their donors and potential donors. In addition to what they store in terms of dollar amounts given, they store lots of other stuff that's related to whether or not they give, how much, how often. Like that.

Peter: (as the light went on) So you can build models with multiple regression …

Bo: That's just one way. I prefer neural networks …

Peter: Yeah, but whatever technique you select, you can build a score that tells you how likely they are to give, how often, and so on.

Bo: That's it.

Peter: Youda man, Bo.

Bo: Everybody knows that.

From that point on, I haven't really wanted to do anything professionally other than what Bo had so succinctly described on that fall day all those years ago.

Rachel Pollack. In November of 1998 I sent a draft of an article I had written on how data mining and predictive modeling might be used by academic fundraisers to Rachel, who was then an editor at CASE's magazine, CURRENTS. I had just found her name on the web; I had only the vaguest idea of what CASE and its mission was. Rachel liked the article.

In April of 1999 it appeared as "Model Behavior: Statistical modeling can help you find the right equation for annual fund success." Thanks to Rachel, I've had a long and enjoyable relationship with CASE. The book you're reading is part of that.

Working as a volunteer data miner. By 1999 my financial situation had gotten to the point where I didn't really need to make much money for Linda and me to live a comfortable, albeit moderate, life style. To get things moving on the work front, I simply started volunteering my data-mining services to schools and nonprofits. Most of them were taken aback; but they quickly saw it as a sort of in-kind gift, and many of them accepted my offer. It was a good deal for me, and it was a good deal for them. I got my hands on a lot of data, and I learned a ton from analyzing it.

2000–Present

This has been a fun time for me. I'm working with John Sammis (a fantastic partner) on teaching people to do data mining or doing it directly for their institutions. I'm writing this book with a guy who is even more committed (if that's possible) to this sort of work than I am. And I will not stop doing it until my mind gives out. I'm a happy boy. It doesn't mean that I'm not often frustrated by people who should get this stuff but don't. But I am far more heartened than frustrated. Why? Because you're reading this book. Simple as that.

And Kevin's thoughts:

It seems nothing in my early life or job experience could have predicted that I would end up working with data for a living. I barely passed Grade 12 math and never took math or stats again. On the other hand, once you know where a story is headed, it's human nature to go back and find the details that make the outcome seem inevitable. I didn't enjoy math in school, but that may have had more to do with school than with math. As a child I had a book called *Mathemagic*. There are a few books by that name, but this was part of a series of books that are probably no longer around. To my school-conditioned mind, this book couldn't really have been about math because it was too fun. My siblings and I spent hours cutting out flat paper shapes that we copied out of this book and then folded and glued into three-dimensional forms, from simple cubes to dodecahedrons—a polyhedron with 12 faces. Challenging for a kid with small fingers and not a lot of patience, but the results were very cool, and who knew we were learning geometry?

Then there were the number tricks. You might be familiar with this one: If you multiply 9 by any regular whole number, and repeatedly add the digits of the answer until it is just one digit, you will end up with 9. For example, 42 times 9 equals 378. Then add 3 + 7 + 8, which equals 18, and 1 + 8 equals 9. You can do that with any number and the result is the same. This doesn't work with any other digit. I could not understand what was so special about the number 9, so I spent many hours with paper or chalkboard multiplying astronomically huge numbers by 9, and adding the digits of the result, hoping to find an exception. I never succeeded, because the answer was always (and always will be) 9. I was having fun with numbers, yet in school I struggled through math problems I didn't care about. It wasn't that the school problems had no obvious point—it was that I didn't get to choose the problems. It was only later in life, when I began to tackle challenges of my own choosing, that math and statistics suddenly became as absorbing as this number game once was.

During my childhood, the old technologies of numbers and statistics were joined by new technologies for handling them faster and faster, and in ever-greater volume. I was mostly unaware of all that, but in the mid-1980s, my friends and I were avid users of early home computers. I had a Commodore Vic-20 (and later a Commodore 64), with which I learned some rudimentary programming in BASIC. My friends were sprinting ahead of me in that department, however, and feeling that I could not keep up, I decided against pursuing computer science after high school in favor of my other interest, which was writing.

I graduated with a bachelor's degree in journalism in 1991, and went off to write and edit for newspapers and magazines. Computers were just starting to take over in journalism and publishing, so like most people I learned to use technology strictly as a requirement of employment. Over the next dozen years, I wrote for farming and forestry magazines, freelanced a bit, and traveled around Canada for most of a year before landing a job editing a commercial fishing trade magazine on the Pacific coast. Along the way I edited a book, created a website for a weekly newspaper that had employed me as a student, and co-hosted a jazz radio program with my wife, Leslie. My experience was growing increasingly varied, but I don't recall being much interested in data or messing around on a computer.

I was back home on the east coast, self-employed as a writer and editor, when I received a call from someone I knew at nearby St. Francis Xavier University in Antigonish, Nova Scotia. They needed a writer in their advancement department to fill in for a communications staff person on maternity leave. Not really cut out for the discipline of self-employment and tired of meager earnings, I gladly signed up for a regular paycheck. To my surprise, I found that I loved working in advancement. Every morning I looked forward to spending the day on this quiet, small-town university campus. I was fortunate to have my year term extended a couple of times, and then I made a most unexpected switch: A position came open in the development office for a prospect researcher, and I took it. I didn't really know what a prospect researcher was supposed to do, nor if I would like it. But I learned quickly and embraced the notion of helping to unite institutional needs with the interests of prospective donors, at the right level of support. Over the next five years, I not only grew into the position, but I changed it—redefining what the prospect researcher had always done.

The university had a history of strong alumni support. But it was also clear that there were many alumni who were not giving as much as they could. It wasn't that they were reluctant to increase their commitment; they simply hadn't been asked. As with many institutions, we were doing a good job at the major-gift level and at the entry-gift level via the annual fund. But in between was a huge gap that was underdeveloped, with no one specifically tasked to address it.

The first job was to identify who could be approached to give at significantly higher levels. Our vice president of advancement, Peter Fardy, was convinced that the answer would be found in our data—our history of gift transactions with our more than 30,000 living alumni. The challenge was passed to me to think on, and so I was introduced to my first business problem with a data solution.

I dove in, poring over massive spreadsheets with columns of giving totals for a dozen past fiscal years. I started thinking about ways to identify patterns of giving that indicated someone was on a trajectory to bigger things. I stumbled around seeking help from people in my department. The way I was asking my questions must have triggered something in the mind of one co-worker, who handed me her copy of *Data Mining for Fund Raisers*, written by another guy named Peter—in this case, Peter Wylie. I read it and was instantly intrigued. The concept of data mining, totally foreign to me up to that point, was clearly explained and seemed uniquely suited to what we were trying to get at. I read the book a second time, and I also started posting questions to listservs such as Prospect-L, trying to tie what I had read to the problem I had in front of me.

One day, my phone rang and who should be on the other end but Peter Wylie himself. I was to learn that reaching out by phone was very much his way, but at the time I was startled to suddenly be speaking with the guy who wrote this awesome little book that I had become such a fan of. Peter worked with me to show how we could get smart about using our data. It took a year—he had created a predictive score for us, which we hadn't used but were able to test against actual results. Thus armed with evidence, I was able to convince my manager that we needed to invest in one-on-one training. It was only then that I was able to translate Peter's straightforward method to precise steps in a software package.

What did training accomplish that working on my own could not?

- One, the training was couched in the language of fundraising, not statistics. Terms from statistics were introduced as needed, and selectively. A comprehensive understanding of stats was not the goal.

- Two, it was specific to the software that I was actually using (Data Desk). This allowed every step to be as concrete as "Next, click on the Manip menu and select … ." I was shown how to use the small set of software features that I really needed, and we ignored the rest.

- Three, it was specific to my own data. I learned through the process of building a model for our own institution, with data pulled from our own database. It was the first time I had seen our alumni and donation data presented this way. If we had never proceeded to full-on data mining, I still would have learned a lot about our constituency.

After that I never looked back. I found the subject completely absorbing. For every new concept I learned, there were five more waiting to be discovered. New applications for data mining kept occurring to me. I had never been so excited by work. When Peter learned that I had been a writer, he suggested I ought to write some discussion papers, as he had been doing with his partner, John Sammis. But I started a blog instead, which I called CoolData, a name I came up with in five minutes, in December of 2009. The blog brought me in contact with experts in the field, some of whom went on to write guest posts—including a few by Peter Wylie himself—and has been a key element in my own continuing education. Visited by more than a thousand people from around the world every week, CoolData has led to new friendships, a lot of knowledge exchange, and invitations to present at conferences all over North America. It's been way more fun than I ever expected.

Eventually I left St. Francis Xavier University, where I had learned so much as a prospect researcher, and Leslie and I moved to the city of Halifax, where I started a new job at Dalhousie University, a larger institution, with a bigger database, and new, complex challenges. Data mining and predictive modeling are now core functions of my position. What was once a side-interest is now my full-time job.

I would like to say that I got to this point via my own initiative, but that would be wrong. A little earlier, my co-author talked about brakes and accelerators. I've been fortunate to have many accelerators along the way. It took one Peter to recognize that the way to unlocking greater value in our development programs was through our data, and then to challenge a somewhat under-qualified staffer (me) to think about how to approach those problems. And it took another Peter to bend my head around the concepts and to continue to mentor me long after our training sessions were over. Many others helped me along the way so that I could query the database and understand what all those codes meant. My co-workers and experts on the Prospect-DMM listserv answered one dumb question after another. Even the blog wasn't my idea—Leslie came up with that.

Some of my happiest moments occur when I am working. I could never have said that before I discovered my interest in data and being introduced to the tools to work with it. My work provides plenty of challenges, and sometimes I get stuck for days, but the feeling that my skills are a good match for the difficulty brings great satisfaction to making incremental progress on big problems. What I do happens to be of value to my employer, of course—otherwise how would I get paid to play all day? A paycheck is one of the external reasons I do what I do. The internal reasons, the reasons that are harder to explain but which probably best account for my motivation to continue making progress, have to do with challenges that are significant but surmountable, a high degree of personal growth in meeting those challenges, and just the elegance and fun of the tools I use. I ENJOY dragging variable icons across the screen in Data Desk into my regression analysis, and watching all the numbers change, and thinking about why they change.

People who ask us questions about how to get into data mining tend to be concerned with acquiring hard skills. From what we've said here, you can tell we put more stress on soft skills—enjoyment, even passion. We urge institutions to embrace analytics because it's important and good, but our message to you, the individual, is different: We urge you to embrace working with data if it's something that gives you joy. In his book *Flow: The Psychology of Optimal Experience*, Mihaly Csikszentmihalyi distinguishes between intrinsic and extrinsic motivation. Being intrinsically motivated means that you do something, not for reward or for an ultimate purpose (which are extrinsic motivators), but for the simple enjoyment of doing. If you find pleasure in working with the numbers and concepts of data mining, or in using the software tools you have, you will probably be motivated toward increased personal growth in that direction, picking up hard skills as you go.

Our stories should also lead you to understand that statistics and computer software are just the tools and outward appearance of the work that we do. The true enjoyment happens in the mind, as with any type of work that is fulfilling. Unfortunately, too many people have grown up convinced that numbers and charts are beyond them. As a society we rightly place a high value on literacy— few people today would brag that they have no ability or interest in reading. Yet many people are happy to confess their hopelessness with numbers or math. As citizens, taxpayers and voters, and consumers of news media and health care services, our collective ignorance about statistics does us no favors—we are the fool of anyone wielding a chart.

That can change. In the meantime, there is no reason to allow incorrect assumptions about your lack of ability to work competently with numbers (and enjoy it, too) to stop you.

For anyone looking to break into analytics as a career, would formal education in computing and programming (or statistics and advanced mathematics, or business, or database-related information technology) be a big asset? Well, sure. If you're young and prepared for years of university, and already have a bent in any of these directions, then go for it. But don't let yourself be steered into subject areas that are not of central interest to you. Analytics may be best pursued as complimentary to work that interests you—as a means of doing great work in a new, insightful way.

In other words, if you want to work with data, then just do it. Look around you, where you are working right now. Seek out any sort of data-related problem or project you can find in your current employment, and learn just enough to make some progress. Any exposure to real-world data and its messy problems will be good experience.

As Peter concludes: "If you really want to do this stuff, you'll find a way just as Kevin and I have. You will. And once you get to where you want to be and somebody comes along and really wants to do the same thing, help them out as best you can. Be an accelerator. Don't be a brake. They'll find enough brakes on their own."

Lessons Learned in the Field: Final Words from Peter

Kevin asked me to write about some of the lessons I've learned from working in data analytics over the last decade and a half. I hope you can take advantage of things I've learned (often the hard way) and learn them far earlier in your career than I did. Much of this is personal rather than technical, so I understand if you skip over it. But I hope you don't.

Here's the list:

- There is no intellectual activity I enjoy more than analyzing data.
- I'm always ready to be humbled by what I don't know.
- Scholarly books and articles are badly written, but I should read some of them anyway.
- I should ask for help from people who are skilled in areas where I am clumsy or downright inept.
- Things move at a snail's pace in the world of advancement, but the really nice people in the field balance it out for me.

There is no intellectual activity I enjoy more than analyzing data.
I grew up as a kid who continually got the message: "Being good at things is what matters most in life. Get good grades, get into a first-rate college, be really skilled at whatever sports you play, write well, be a captivating speaker … " The list goes on and on. And maybe the list is not so bad. Maybe it's that I didn't make up the list, and I didn't get to do the judging of how good I was at the things on the list. I hope you have not (and will not) spend all the time I've spent feeling bad because I simply wasn't good enough at something I "should" be good at. It's a bloody waste of time.

As I've gotten older I have to come to believe that being good at stuff is not all that important. What's important is loving what I do, not whether I'm particularly good at it or not. For me, if it's a physical activity, hitting tennis balls is what I love the most, not beating someone in a game. Just the joy of moving around the court and trying to get the ball back to my hitting partner so he or she can send the fuzzy yellow sphere back one more time so I can whack it again.

Intellectually, there is nothing that captivates me, that transports me, the way analyzing data does. For many years, I had hoped that writing would provide that kind of complete absorption. It doesn't, although sometimes it comes close. For the most part, writing is a chore. It's something I do because it helps me express my ideas and thoughts. But it doesn't pull me up to the laptop and draw me into the sanctum the way looking for answers with data does. And I feel enormously grateful that I know this.

I'm always ready to be humbled by what I don't know.
I've learned to speak French quite fluently. On a recent trip to Paris and the Loire Valley, I had occasion to speak to lots of francophones whose English was extremely limited. Time after time, they would tell me how impressed they were with my facility with their language. I would thank them and then say, "The more I know, the more I don't know."

They understood. They knew that as much as I might learn about their tongue, I would never know its breadth and depth the way they know it. They knew they could use idioms and argot and expressions in talking to me, and I would have to stop and say, "What does that mean?" They, of course, saw no shame in that. I don't think I did either, but I did feel humbled and maybe a little bit embarrassed by my ignorance.

Well, that's just tough. That's the way a broad and deep knowledge base is. I'm not going to get my hands around but a small part of it, whether it's a language or statistics and data analysis. And I can put up with the constant humbling and mild embarrassment when my ignorance stares at me. In fact, those frequent discoveries motivate me to learn more about what I would so like to master but never will.

Scholarly books and articles are badly written, but I should read some of them anyway.
When I was in high school and (for a while) in college, I would read something and think, "Well, I guess I should understand this, but I don't. Maybe I'm not smart enough to understand it." But as I got a little older and more confident in my own writing, I decided, "No, the problem is not me. This thing (book or article) is badly written. What editor let this get into print?"

Well, things haven't changed much since my youth. Most scholarly writing is lousy, and it doesn't make reading the stuff any fun. On the other hand, I do think wading through some of that scholarly writing on data analytics and methodology is worth the effort. First I'll tell you why, then offer some tips on how to make the process easier.

- **You'll learn stuff you didn't know about and should**. This happens to me all the time. For example, I'm very comfortable with a technique called multiple regression; I grew up with it from my years in graduate school. But there are other multivariate techniques that I'm not very familiar with at all. One of these used to be logistic regression. I am certainly not an expert on it now, but I'd be woefully ignorant about it if I hadn't waded through some pretty heavy material on the topic. And it took more than a few book chapters and articles for me to get my arms around the subject. More important, the reading got me to actually use logistic regression, and use it a lot.

- **You'll learn where there are big gaps in the research literature that badly need filling**. A while back I helped someone on her dissertation having to do with data mining in higher education. As with all dissertations, there was an exhaustive review of the literature. And I mean exhaustive. Yes, most of it was horribly written. No surprise there. What *was* a surprise was that the vast majority of the scholarly pieces she reviewed were based on *survey* data! Survey data that was gathered ignoring all kinds of methodological principles. That got my attention. So reading all that "material" (boring enterprise that it was) was worth it.

- **You'll get ideas you wouldn't have otherwise gotten**. Here's an example that goes back to my grad school days. Back then the Institute of Social Research at the University of Michigan was putting out a lot of monographs on new ways to analyze data. (It still does.) The monographs were actually quite readable. I remember one in particular called AID (Automatic Interaction Detector). Interactions were something I was very interested in at the time (still am).[1] Well, this monograph showed a very commonsensical branching technique to discover interactions. The piece was clearly written, and it showed how the more traditional techniques available at the time for finding interactions missed a lot. I still have that monograph.

Now some tips on making the reading process easier:

- **Look for books designed to "dumb" things down for us**. Everybody knows about these books. I don't like the term *dumb down*, but these books tend to be very reader friendly and understandable. There are a lot of them out there for people who feel uncomfortable with more standard, academic texts.

- **Surf the web for free stuff on analytics.** I don't suspect you need any convincing that the advent of the Internet has fundamentally changed our lives. What you may not be aware of, however, is the huge amount of material available free for downloading that ties into the work we do. Here's an example of something I found that I'm still wading through as of this writing: "A Conversation with Leslie Kish," by Martin Frankel, and Benjamin King.[2] Leslie Kish is the author of a classic text on survey sampling that I had in a course on survey research in grad school long ago. A fascinating man, and the document goes on for almost 25 pages. It is not easy reading all the way through, but anybody involved in doing or purchasing a web survey should read it. I've also downloaded an entire chapter of a book that is out of print. The chapter is on scaling and it goes on for more than 150 detailed pages. Again, not something to be devoured like a racy mystery or suspense novel. But there is much to be gleaned from it. I'm gleaning … at a snail's pace.

- **Store everything you can on a tablet**. I have an iPad. I love it. But there are plenty of alternatives. The point is that a tablet is far more convenient for casual reading than a laptop. You don't have to take it out of the case when you go through security at the airport. You can stuff it in a backpack or briefcase and break it out when you have a free moment. And free moments are a good time to read the kind of material I'm talking about. I'm good for maybe 10 minutes, and then it's time to do something else like read the novel I also have stored on the device or check the weather where I'd rather be right now or whatever.

I should ask for help from people who are skilled in areas where I am clumsy or downright inept.

I'm not a particularly good parallel parker. My wife, Linda, is very skilled at parallel parking. So if we're in a hurry to find a parking spot and get to a movie or meet up with people, I will often see a spot that I'm pretty sure I couldn't get the car into. I'll say, "Can you handle that?" "Yep." I hop out, and she hops in behind the wheel and slides the car in with consummate ease.

Your fragile ego won't park a car, and it won't get you unstuck from an analytical problem. It's okay to admit when you don't know how. Otherwise learning will be far more difficult than it has to be.

Things move at a snail's pace in the world of advancement, but the really nice people in the field balance it out for me.

I am not good at dealing with difficult people (and I count myself among them), people whose phones always go to voicemail, who don't return calls or emails, unappreciative people incapable of saying "thank you." There are people working in advancement who are not warm and welcoming. Ours is a people business, but every week I encounter advancement professionals who don't seem to embrace that concept.

Is the field filled with difficult people? Quite to the contrary, I see our field as filled with caring, dedicated folks who are fun to be around. Far too many of them let me keep them on the phone with my corny jokes and stories when they should be telling me to stop talking and let them get back to work. They bring light and levity into my life every day I get a chance to interact with them.

Yeah, they work for places that take a long time to get things done. It's okay. I can live with that.

---

1. Very briefly, *interaction* is a term used in analysis of variance and multiple regression to denote a relationship between two variables that differs as a function of another variable. For example, there may be a strong relationship between a verbal SAT score and GPA for one ethnic group, but not for another.
2. *Statistical Science* 11, no. 1 (1996): 65–87. Available at http://bit.ly/Myi9lx

chapter 5

Some Data Essentials

any people who work in fundraising, and the related professions that support and surround them, deal with data every day. Annual giving staff, prospect researchers, gift processing staff, alumni records staff, and IT and computing staff—all have their own interactions with data, whether creating it, entering it, maintaining it, extracting it, shaping it, presenting it, or interpreting it. All have their own views about what "it" really is. And all of those views may be slightly at odds with how a predictive modeler sees data.

In this chapter you will learn about new ways of looking at your data, not just as a collection of discrete facts that you pull from as needed—like looking up a phone number or summing up a column in a spreadsheet report—but as a continuous whole in which you discover useful patterns and connections you may not have suspected even existed. This approach might be new to you even if you work with data in a highly technical way every day. As we'll show you, analysis is less about techie stuff than it is about grasping some basic concepts.

How much do you need to know about statistics? Peter has been a student of statistics for more than 40 years. He's taken lots of statistics courses. He's read dozens of books on various aspects of statistics. He did his doctoral dissertation on a statistical topic (one that would put you right to sleep). He's tutored lots of students who were struggling with the topic. And he uses statistics just about every day in his work as he trains advancement professionals to do data mining and predictive modeling.

You, on the other hand, are likely to be more like Kevin. You are most likely not a statistics expert. What's more, you probably don't want—or need—to be one. You need only the essentials, without being burdened with details, terms, and techniques you don't have to know and aren't likely to use. We hope to impart some of the essentials in this chapter: just enough of the basics so that if you want to start analyzing your database with one of the statistical software packages out there, you'll have a clearer sense of what the software can do and how to approach the data.

Some of the differences in the way we think about and describe the data are merely ones of terminology; we will deal with those in a minute. Some differences have to do with how data is viewed by the discipline of statistics—differences that are partly terminology and partly conceptual. We'll get into that, too. Finally, there are differences that are fundamental; and although they may seem "only" philosophical, these differences are perfectly real and carry practical consequences. We will discuss these first.

This Data Is Different

At its most basic, the distinction is this: There is "everyday" data—generated by processing gifts, updating constituent records, maintaining databases, and pulling reports—and "insight" data, the data we use for predictive modeling. Actually, it's the same data; what is different is how we think about it. Both everyday data and insight data are important, but they differ in their purposes, quality, and content.

Purposes. Everyday data is used for sense-making and explaining in the present, via the reporting and descriptive statistics that we associate with business intelligence (BI). A typical example of a question that would be answered in the world of everyday data might be: "What were December's gift totals, and how do they compare with the same period last year?" The purpose is to report, explain, and describe what has occurred in the past, or to describe what is happening in the present in comparison to what happened in the past. Insight, or modeling, data, on the other hand, is not reporting or explaining anything. When we build models, we are seeking to uncover useful associations between things ("Is there a connection between giving in December and being a significant donor?"). Then we use those associations to predict what will happen in the future.

Quality. When everyday data is messy, it will probably be dismissed as invalid. An address list won't get used for a mailing if a lot of the records contain errors. When modeling data is messy, that's considered normal, and there are techniques to address it. For everyday data, missing values are an issue; for modeling data, missing values can be useful, (i.e., predictive). When missing data is troublesome rather than predictive, we are free to make approximations to help fill the gaps. "Making up data" is a foreign concept to people who deal exclusively with everyday data.

Content. In the everyday, we are picky: "Give me these records, but not those, and include this field and this field, but not those fields." For modeling, we say, "Give me everything—I want it all!" Everyday data seeks an answer, a single-point destination reached by one route. Modeling data has a destination too, but it gets there via a myriad of routes. Every potential predictor is a new route to explore. And we don't know in advance what routes will get us there fastest; we have to drive them all. The content difference is also temporal: In the everyday, the most current data supersedes and replaces old data. Think again of address information: Of what use is a mailing list to the alumni office if it's full of addresses from the 1970s? Well, in modeling, that old data can be just as valuable as fresh data. For example, the number of address updates an individual has provided to the institution over a lifetime of being an alum may be highly predictive of giving. The only way we can get that count is if we total up the number of records, both active and inactive. No historical records, no predictor.

Data is not just information, which is how someone in gift processing or alumni records might see data. Yes, we can look up an individual's address and phone number, but we can do a whole lot more besides. And data is not just part of the technology, which is how someone in IT might see it. Servers and hard drives are replaceable, but data is not. The cost of acquiring and maintaining data may be high, but because data has uses we can't foresee, and because it cannot be recovered once deleted, its value cannot even be calculated. Data is also something other than just monitoring or reporting or describing via statistics.

For us, data is an open field in which fresh discoveries may be made—now, or years from now. Data, therefore, is a core asset of your institution, at least as valuable as buildings and any physical infrastructure. It requires safeguarding and protection, for exploration into the future. When an institution fails to protect this asset, bad things can happen, such as:

1. Data that would be useful to have is never captured or entered.
2. Historical data is overwritten with newer data.
3. Data is deliberately deleted or is left out of a database conversion.

Some of these bad things unfurl slowly and unnoticed over years, while others happen with the click of a mouse. The result is the same: Key insights into engagement are lost forever. Every annual fund donor who will never be proactively identified as a major gift or planned giving prospect is a huge loss. Institutional memory is flushed away, harming not just data-mining efforts but prospect research and other data-related work. *Disaster* is not too strong a word to describe the financial impact of the accumulation of such losses. It's a hidden disaster, too. No one will ever be able to add up the cost of what's been lost collectively by the schools and nonprofits that have failed to safeguard one of their most precious assets.

Some institutions have never bothered to capture key engagement-related data such as athletic team or campus club membership in their databases. For institutions without yearbooks, that's a total loss. Others have development offices that fail to force gift officers to file contact reports. Future staff (new university presidents included) face being embarrassed by their lack of knowledge of prospects' previous meetings, tours of campus, or gift asks—but the pain of embarrassment might be just the tip of the iceberg. Organizations outside the realm of higher ed, even very large ones, are especially prone to neglect gathering data.

Then there are institutions with a penchant for overwriting historical data with current data: deleting old addresses when mail is returned or new addresses are found, for example. The worst instance of this we've heard about is one school that wiped out all data related to an alum's original degree whenever a graduate returned for post-grad work or a higher degree. A much more common issue is failing to protect historical fundraiser prospect assignments, an important aspect of a person's history of their relationship with an institution. In at least one case we know of, such overwriting was deemed necessary in order for information to come out properly on reports—a case of the technology tail wagging the strategy dog.

Most distressing, however, are the cases of entire databases being destroyed. Here are a few examples collected anonymously from universities across the United States.

- "The database had serious size limitations, so in order to free up space, all records marked deceased were deleted. Some old gift data also was deleted, I think (all older than seven years at the time of deletion, since apparently someone thought we only needed seven years of info). The result was that we lost some irreplaceable information, particularly in trying to track down relatives of individuals who made estate gifts or endowments, since the original records (with attached names, contact reports, etc.) were purged."

- "Due to limited database space, this organization did indeed perform a huge purge of information sometime in the early '90s. Luckily, there was someone cognizant enough regarding historical values to not allow any purging of gifts. However, many never-givers' records and parents of alumni records were all purged from the system with all of the notes and information in those records. In addition, many historical addresses were purged. Someone decided that only ONE former address for each record was necessary!"

- One university established in the 1930s, which is on its third database for registration and alumni records, has been committing a variety of data crimes that include overwriting and deleting. During database conversions the following things have occurred: Those who attended but did not receive a degree were never transferred to the new database; the records of alumni who held certain types of degrees were never transferred from paper to digital format and are not in the database; people who died or had no valid address were not uploaded to the newer databases; and, finally, someone overwrote all the female constituent's middle names with maiden names when they married. The contributor who sent this list added, "One of the older databases that still had some of the old missing data crashed and IT was going to just forget about it. I begged for the tables from this database and built an Access database so we could at least query and lookup this old data, otherwise it would have disappeared."

Advancement services and IT staff are the professionals who keep our data ship afloat, and we do not mean to suggest that these horror stories represent typical operating procedure. Moreover, many of the worst disasters we know about happened 10 years ago or more. Consciousness about the value of historical data is on the rise, and we can hope that cases such as this are becoming increasingly rare.

It is possible to both protect the integrity of the data for today's use and ensure that it remains intact for analysis years from now. Documented standards and procedures for data entry that are rigorously enforced can prevent errors from being committed in the first place. Regular communication among all data users is a must. Anything involving the moving or altering of large portions of data must involve consultation, and it must proceed according to a plan. No one person should make unilateral decisions about this important asset.

Different Data, Different Terms

The source of much of the data you will use in modeling is likely a relational database, perhaps a very complex one such as many universities use, with hundreds of interconnecting tables forming a multidimensional structure. In contrast, the essential structure for data as we will analyze it is relatively simple: a single file that is "flat"—that is, all the relationships in the data have been re-expressed into only two dimensions. Data that you extract from your database, or have pulled for you, is always in this form. As anyone knows who's used a spreadsheet program such as Excel, those dimensions are called rows and columns, and its shape is a rectangle. Table 5.1 shows you what a typical Excel spreadsheet looks like.

In analysis we have different names for these rows and columns. Each spreadsheet row is a *record*, and each column is a *variable*. Typically the data sets we work with contain one row (record) for each individual (uniquely identified by an ID number), and each row contains data pertaining to that individual. A lot of the work of preparing a data file for analysis involves ensuring that we have just one record for each individual.

When we start to analyze our data statistically using software, we will refer to each record as a *case*. As we get further along in this book, whenever we refer to cases, we are really talking about records or individuals.

An individual could be any constituent in our database—alumni, donors, members, companies, foundations—but normally we do not analyze persons and non-persons in the same data file. In all the examples used in this book, our data sets are made up exclusively of people who are constituents of our databases, are not marked "deceased," and, usually, are also contactable in some way, whether by phone, mail, or email.

If our data file contains alumni donors, for example, we say that the *unit of analysis* is the individual alum. The unit of analysis is simply the entity on which we focus our study. We could, if we wanted, do statistical analysis of individual

TABLE 5.1 The Format of an Excel Spreadsheet

ID	TOTAL_AMT	PREF_YR	MAJOR	DOB	GENDER	MARITAL_STATUS	NUM_CHILDREN
A000037067	4,565.00	1976	Accounting		M	Married	1
A000037069	1,284.00	1976	Mechanical Engineering		M	Married	2
A000037073	5.00	1976	Chemical Engineering		F	Married	
A000037075	918.34	1976	Chemistry		M	Married	2
A000037077	595.00	1976	Business Administration		M	Married	5
A000037080	3,490.00	1976	Mathematics		M	Married	3
A000047081	0.00	1976	Electrical Engineering		M	Unmarried	
A000047085	1,130.00	1976	Mechanical Engineering		M	Unmarried	
A000047090	64,170.00	1976	Chemistry		F	Married	

donations instead of people—in that case, the unit of analysis would be individual gifts. The business intelligence analyst most commonly begins at the level of individual transactions when building a report. But in the behavioral modeling we are doing in this book, the entities we are studying and scoring are always individual people, with one row defining all the attributes of a single person.

When we pull data from the database for analysis, we need to form our queries with the issue of duplicate records in mind. For example, if we ask for all constituents' phone numbers and don't specify that we want only the person's *preferred* number, then Joe Smith might appear three times, once each with his home number, his business number, and his mobile number.

Of course, in modeling we don't usually care what a person's actual number is, but we do care about the fact of having (or not having) a phone number, and we might also care about the number of phone numbers (current and historical) we have in the database for an individual. Therefore, we query the database for the presence of *any* number (a Yes or No condition), or for a *count* of numbers (resulting in a single count for each person). If we wanted, we could also ask for a Yes/No variable (or count) for each type of phone number (home, business, and mobile), resulting in three phone-related variables instead of one. The end result is that Joe Smith appears in our data file only once.

A large database may contain dozens of people named Joe Smith, maybe even several Joseph N. Smiths with an address in New York, NY. We trust our data entry staff to distinguish between two Joseph N. Smiths who are not the same person and to recognize when in fact they are, such as when the Joe Smith who sends a check for a $100 gift is the same Joe Smith who is a member of the Class of 1982.

The piece of data that links records pertaining to the same person—and distinguishes individuals from each other—is called a *unique identifier*. When a student enrolls in a university, she is assigned a student ID and will carry it for the rest of her life as an alumna and, we hope, a donor. In fact, even after she dies her ID will continue to identify her uniquely—it will never (or should never) be assigned to anyone else. The student ID is a familiar example, but *any* database will create unique IDs, often in the form of a number, in order to link an individual's data from one table to another. Any data set pulled from a database for analysis is incomplete if it is missing the unique identifier.

Various Variables

What is a variable? A variable is simply an attribute (such as "gender" or "total dollars given") with values encoded in the form of data. It is "variable" in that the attribute can differ ("vary") from case to case. In our data file for analysis, "ID," or the unique identifier, will always be the first *variable*. Other common variables you will encounter include Lifetime Giving, Age, Home Phone Number, Gender, Marital Status, Number of Events Attended, and Satisfaction Level (which we will explain shortly). We name these variables in particular because they illustrate some of the important ways we distinguish between types of variables in statistics.

First, a variable can be **numeric** or **text**. Lifetime Giving is clearly numeric, and so is Number of Events, while Marital Status is probably text ("M" for married, "S" for single, etc.). Another term for numeric is **quantitative**. Lifetime Giving is a quantitative variable because it contains information about the quantity of something, in this case, dollars and cents.

There are different types of quantitative variables. Lifetime Giving, for example, can range from zero dollars to millions of dollars, and it can take on any value in between. But Number of Events Attended is a "count variable"—it can be zero or any whole number, but one cannot attend 3.5 events. Therefore we refer to Lifetime Giving as a **continuous** variable, and Number of Events as a **discrete** variable. (Variables that are text are by their very nature discrete: For Marital Status, there are no intermediate values between one status and another.)

Sometimes it's not easy to tell if a variable should be called continuous or discrete, and in fact there are no hard and fast rules for distinguishing them. For example, although Lifetime Giving can take any value in the range of zero to millions, the data might be rounded to the nearest whole dollar and could therefore be considered technically discrete. In such cases, common sense must prevail, and we call it continuous. In the case of Age, we also impose discrete categories on a continuous variable, but we still usually think of Age as continuous. Your choice may depend on the type of analysis you happen to be doing.

What about Home Phone Number? It may be numeric, but it is not quantitative—it is composed of digits, but it is not a count or quantity of anything. (In fact, if the phone number contains parentheses or hyphens, we have to treat it as text.) A count of all phone numbers for each ID would be quantitative, and discrete.

In statistics we refer to text variables as **categorical**. A categorical variable can be thought of as a name or label; sometimes, categorical variables are referred to as *nominal*. Gender is categorical: M for male, F for female. Categorical variables don't have to be text: Numeric values may also be categorical, if the number represents a category of something instead of a count or quantity. If all the males in our data set are coded "0" and all the females are coded "1," the variable may be numeric, but it's not quantitative: It is categorical.

The numeric version of the Gender variable is a special kind of categorical variable. When a variable takes on one of only two potential values, we refer to it as a **binary** variable. Usually it is coded as 0/1, and it is very common in predictive modeling. You will also see binary variables referred to as **indicator** variables and **dummy** variables. They all mean the same thing: The variable is a flag that indicates a simple Yes/No condition. (Is the case female, yes or no, 1 or 0?) A key thing about these variables is that it doesn't matter which sex is designated as "1"—there is no quantity of maleness or femaleness being counted up here. It's a category only, and we could just as easily flip it around so that females are 0 and males are 1.

We will see many more examples later in the book, but creating binary variables is a good way to convert certain problematic variables into useful ones. For example, we don't care what the value of Home Phone Number happens to be, but we do care if we HAVE a phone number or not. If we create a new variable that is 1 if a phone number is present and 0 if it is null, that's a useful binary variable we can use in analysis.

In the list of variables above, we added Satisfaction Level as a special example. Think of a survey in which respondents are asked to rate their level of agreement to a statement such as "I would recommend XYZ University to a high school graduate." The levels might be categorical (strongly disagree, somewhat disagree, neutral, somewhat agree, strongly agree) or they might be numeric (0 to 5, with 5 being "strongly agree"), but either way the variable is called **ordinal.** Ordinal (or "scale") data is arranged in a particular order, so that higher values indicate "more" of something than lower values. Any kind of rank is considered ordinal. If we ranked everyone by age and split everyone into 10 equal groups (deciles) from oldest to youngest, that variable would be ordinal. Ordinal data is, strictly speaking, not the same as continuous, quantitative data—it would not be appropriate to calculate the average of an ordinal variable—but the distinction is not always important in predictive modeling. If a variable contains meaning as a rank or scale that approximates a quantity of something, in practice we might treat it like any other quantitative variable.

There's another type of variable we frequently encounter in data mining projects, which we might call "hybrid" variables. As far as we know, *hybrid variable* is not a term you'll find in any statistical or measurement textbook. It's a term Peter made up to deal with variables you'll encounter again and again in the real world. For example, let's look at the variable NUM_CHILDREN, which tells us the number of children the person has listed in the database.

NUM_CHILDREN
1
2
2
5
3

Since it would certainly be reasonable to compute an average for this one, is there any reason we shouldn't call it a quantitative variable? Maybe, but what do we do about the blanks? Do we assume any person with no entry for NUM_CHILDREN has no children and just enter a 0 for that record? That's not a great solution, because we simply don't know what the situation is. All we know is there's nothing listed for the record. So we're much more inclined to code the blanks as "not listed" or "DK" (don't know). And there's the rub. If we do that, then we have a variable that has both numeric and text data from the standpoint of how the statistical software deals with the variable. That is, if we want to compute an average for NUM_CHILDREN, we can only do it for those records that have a number coded; we can't do it for the records that have a code of "not listed" or "DK."

So we end up with a variable that is both quantitative and categorical—a hybrid variable. These don't get talked about in statistics textbooks, but they're definitely a fact of life in the kind of data analysis work we're doing here.

This list of variable types is not exhaustive, but it covers all the important distinctions you will encounter in an analysis or any typical modeling project. If you've learned about statistics in a classroom or from a textbook, most of the examples probably involved quantitative variables. In predictive modeling for fundraising, very few variables are quantitative; aside from Lifetime Giving and Age, almost all the variables you will encounter will either be categorical or a hybrid of quantitative and categorical (to account for data that is missing). This partly explains why statistical methods as presented in textbooks seem so difficult to apply to the real world of your data.

Where Data Comes From

We said earlier that the data used to gain insight into your constituency is the same data generated every day for the institution's regular functions, but looked at in a different way. Here are some suggestions for places to look for variables for analysis you might want to conduct in the future. Many of these hold clues to constituents' level of affinity with your institution.

Degrees

> Graduated (yes/no)
> Number of degrees
> Has degree(s) from another institution
> Class year
> College/Faculty of degree
> Transfer student or received all degree credits from your institution

Name

> Nickname present (yes/no)
> Preferred name present (yes/no)
> Nickname different from Preferred (yes/no)
> First name is in top 10% of popular names (yes/no)
> Prefix present (other than Ms., Mrs., Mr., yes/no)
> Suffix present (yes/no)

Personal and general information

> Age (and/or Class Year)
> Age missing (yes/no)
> Age at graduation
> Sex
> Marital status present (yes/no)
> Marital status (single, married, etc.)
> Recency of update to personal info
> Job title/employer present
> Number of employment updates
> Prominent position (president, CEO, etc.)
> Any family cross-reference present
> Number of family cross-references
> Constituent codes (parent, non-alum spouse, faculty/staff, etc.)

Phone contact history

> Total phonathon talk time (totaled from historical calling projects)
> Total number phonathon call attempts
> Has phonathon pledge refusal reason code
> Number of times phone picked up

Number of times phone failed to pick up
Number of times phonathon "No Pledge"
Number of times bad phone number (Wrong Num, Disconnect)

Contact data

Preferred address type (home, business, etc.)
Home address present (yes/no)
Business address present (yes/no)
Number of address updates
Lives in same city as institution (yes/no)
Lives in same province/state (yes/no)
Lives in USA/Canada/International
Distance from campus
Home phone present
Business phone present
Parent phone present
Has unlisted phone number (yes/no)
Email present (not Gmail, Yahoo, Hotmail)
Email present (Gmail, Yahoo, Hotmail)
Email present (any)
Contact restriction codes

Student activities

Years lived on campus
Greek society membership (yes/no)
Athletics involvement
Campus club/society involvement
Awards, prizes, scholarships or bursaries
Student employment on campus

Alumni activities

Alumni survey responder (yes/no)
Channel of survey response (mail, online, other)
Survey scores (engagement, etc.)
Alumni directory purchaser (yes/no)
Number alumni events/reunions attended
Online community membership or activity
Email for Life account is active (yes/no)
Volunteer activity

Mentorship program activity

Alumni chapter member (yes/no)

Giving

Planned giving expectancy code

Has made a third-party gift (i.e., via business)

Number of third-party gifts

Number of unique gift designations

Has made an in-memory gift

Has made an anonymous gift

Has made an in-honor-of gift

Has made a matched gift

Age at time of first gift

Number of gifts per year

Gift made in form of cash

Gift by check

Business or personal check

Gift made on any credit card

Type of credit card

Has made an in-kind gift

Has made gift of stocks/securities

It would take you a long time to exhaust all the potential sources of interesting data at a large university. And even if you did, many variables can be expressed in different ways and even combined with other variables to make new ones, which vastly multiplies your options. For example, the one data point, "email address" can be turned into any of the following:

- Recency of email address update

- Number of email address updates lifetime

- Number of email address updates divided by years since graduation

- Active email account is an Email for Life address

- Email provider is Gmail, Yahoo, or Hotmail

A lot of the fun in data mining is discovering new variables and new ways to manipulate existing data to discover patterns. For example, as suggested above, it often makes a difference whether an alum's preferred email address is a free account such as Gmail, Yahoo or Hotmail: We've found that it can indicate the alum is less engaged, and less likely to make a gift, than if the email account is not a freebie.

You may have noticed that our list of ideas for variables doesn't include any external data—market research and retail segmentation data, real estate data, demographic and census data, wealth screening data, and so on. There's nothing wrong with analyzing external data if you've got it, but if you're primarily interested in the relationship between your constituency and the institution—that is, affinity, engagement, and likelihood to give—then you should start with the wealth of internal data that you already have. You can probably stop there, too. In our experience, the degree of association between external factors and behaviors such as giving to your institution is relatively weak. A wealth screening rating will give you an idea of capacity, which is extremely useful for donor prospecting but says very little about whether or not that prospect will give a gift.

For many types of data, there is no expiry date when it comes to predictive modeling. For example, old and out-of-date contact information, while useless for just about anything else, is very useful for predicting behaviors. A phone number doesn't have to be valid to be predictive. At some point, that alum provided that number (or email, or cell phone number), and the fact you have it at all is more important than whether you can still reach someone with it.

What about event attendance? We might reasonably assume that an alum who attended a campus event a decade ago and never returned is far less likely to give than someone who visited just last year. Some schools have attendance data going back many years, but is any of that still relevant? The answer is "probably." Kevin once got to study homecoming attendance data for a university that had done a good job of recording it in the database going back 10 years. He already knew that homecoming attendance was predictive of giving for this university but was surprised to discover that one-time, long-ago attendance was equally as predictive as recent attendance. This may not always hold true, of course. But a simple count of event attendance is often a strong data point: Repeat event attendance is very highly associated with giving.

The enemy of relevance when it comes to data isn't how old it is, but how incomplete or biased it is. For example, if you have good data on involvement on athletic teams up until 1985 and then nothing after that—that's a problem. In this case, your variables for athletic involvement will be more informative about how old your alumni are than how engaged they are. If you build a model that is restricted to older alumni, you'll be fine, but if you include the entire database, "athletics" will be highly correlated with "age" and may add little or no predictive value.

Before we move on, one final bit of advice: Analyze your data in the state that you find it. Don't let missing, incomplete, or suspect data stop you from jumping right in and trying to work with it just as it is. You may need to clean it up or manipulate it a bit as you go along, but that does not mean overhauling your database. If your first step is whipping that monster into shape, you'll never get anywhere—it's too much. If you're looking to make a difference and advance the development of analytics in your organization, you should zero in on the biggest question or questions, and don't wait until your data is perfect in order to do so.

In making this point, we are reminded of one of the most common objections we hear to the idea of using contact information variables such as "business phone present" as predictors of behavior: What if some of those numbers are the result of research or data appends, not a result of alumni/donor engagement? Well, sure, if you have additional information about the source of the data, then use it to split the variable to allow for separate testing. But if you don't, why should you assume that the entire project has somehow been invalidated? What a shame if analytics came to a halt based on someone's notions about data purity.

Success in analytics is not an all-at-once deal; it's iterative. It goes like this: "Let's get some kind of answer or focus this year, and through that we'll discover what the valuable data is that we need to augment, improve, or clean up for next time. Then we'll make another, better model next year."

Building a Sample Data File

We've shown you a giant list of potential variables to draw on. Let's back up a bit and show you a data file with far fewer variables. The ones it contains, however, are commonly used for analysis, and they'll be enough to get you started. (This example is drawn from Peter's earlier book, *Data Mining for Fund Raisers,* published by CASE in 2004. This book remains one of the clearest expositions of the basic ideas behind predictive modeling for a higher-education advancement audience, and for that reason it is still in demand and worth reading on its own as an approachable introduction to the field.)

If you are relying on someone in IT to pull the data for you, then you might not want to ask for everything plus the kitchen sink. The IT person is busy enough, and you'll want to stay on her good side.

Here are some suggested fields you can ask her to include in the Excel file. You can also see how each field might look in Excel for the first nine records. Don't worry if some of these data elements are not available (not everyone has data on the number of children their alumni have, for example). Just get what you can.

ID: The unique number that the institution uses to identify each record in its database.

ID
00000037067
00000037069
00000037073
00000037075
00000037077
00000037080
00000047081
00000047085
00000047090

TOTAL_AMT: The total dollars each individual has given the institution since that person's record has been in the database.

TOTAL_AMT
4,565.00
1,284.00
5.00
918.34
595.00
3,490.00
0.00
1,130.00
64,170.00

PREF_YR: The graduating class that the person (if a former student) prefers to be associated with. In this case, it seems that the database starts with a large group of records for the class of 1976. That doesn't mean 1976 is the oldest class in the database, just that its ID numbers happen to come first. The order of the records doesn't make a difference to us.

PREF_YR
1976
1976
1976
1976
1976
1976
1976
1976
1976

MAJOR: The undergraduate major of the person (if a former student).

MAJOR
Accounting
Mechanical Engineering
Chemical Engineering
Chemistry
Business Administration
Mathematics
Electrical Engineering
Mechanical Engineering
Chemistry

DOB: The day, month, and year of the person's birth. Here we show the first 12 records (rather than the first nine) because this field is so sparsely populated.

DOB
16-Jan-55
24-Feb-55

GENDER: Whether the person is male or female. Limit this field to current sex for transgendered alumni, if your institution creates a new record instead of over-writing the former sex.

GENDER
M
M
F
M
M
M
M
M
F

MARITAL_STATUS: Whether the person is listed as "divorced," "married," "single," "surviving spouse," or "unmarried."

MARITAL_STATUS
Married
Married
Married
Married
Married
Married
Unmarried
Unmarried
Married

NUM_CHILDREN: The number of children the person has listed in the database.

NUM_CHILDREN
1
2
2
5
3

FRAT: Whether or not the person (if a former student) belonged to a fraternity or sorority while an undergraduate at the institution. Notice that our IT person has only indicated a "Y" (for yes) if the person was definitely listed as having belonged to a fraternity or sorority. A blank means either that the person was not a "Greek" member or that we don't know.

FRAT
Y
Y

STUD_ORG: Whether or not the person (if a former student) belonged to at least one student organization while an undergraduate or a graduate student. A blank means either that the person was not a member or that we don't know.

STUD_ORG
Y
Y
Y
Y

HOME_PHONE: Whether or not the person has a home phone listed in the database. Notice that she has not indicated an "N" for "no phone listed." That's something we need to ask her about.

HOME_PHONE
Y
Y
Y
Y
Y
Y
Y
Y

BUS_PHONE: Whether or not the person has a business phone listed in the database. Notice that none of the first nine records listed in the Excel file has a business phone listed. It's a good hunch that this is a far more sparsely populated field than HOME_PHONE.

BUS_PHONE

JOB_TITLE: Whether or not the person has a job title listed in the database.

JOB_TITLE
Y
Y
Y
Y
Y
Y
Y

EMAIL: Whether or not the person has an email address listed in the database.

EMAIL
Y
Y
Y
Y
Y
Y

Ways to Summarize Variables

Earlier we introduced you to two different types of variables—categorical and quantitative—and we talked about the idea of a hybrid variable. Now we can talk about some ways to summarize these variables. But first let's discuss why summarizing variables is a good thing to do. Once again, we are borrowing these examples from Peter's book *Data Mining for Fund Raisers*.

Consider the variable MARITAL_STATUS, which indicates whether the person is listed as "divorced," "married," "single," "surviving spouse," "unmarried," or "widowed." Here's how the first nine records looked:

MARITAL_STATUS
Married
Married
Married
Married
Married
Married
Unmarried
Unmarried
Married

Imagine looking at this variable as a field in Excel. If we scroll down through the thousands of records in the file, we'll see entries for "divorced," "married," "single," and so on slide by. While it's useful to glance at all this raw data to get a sense of how it's stored, it's very hard to get our arms around all those entries. But what if we constructed a table like Table 5.2, which shows the frequencies and percentages of each marital code in our data file? In this example, the file is a sample of about 5,000 records chosen at random from a much larger database.

All of a sudden what was a mass of data becomes a little easier to get some perspective on. At a glance, we can learn a number of facts about our database:

- Almost 60% of the records list "married."

- About 40% list "unmarried."

- The other categories (as a total) constitute less than one-half of 1% of our database.

Those are facts. Nobody can dispute them unless they find an error in our computations. But a summary like this does more than reveal facts. It stimulates interesting questions. For example, in this project we're on a hunt for predictors

TABLE 5.2 Frequencies and Percentages of Marital Codes in Data File

MARITAL STATUS	COUNT	%
Divorced	8	0.16
Married	2,935	58.87
Single	2	0.04
Surviving Spouse	1	0.02
Unmarried	2,031	40.73
Widowed	9	0.18
Total	**4,986**	**100.00**

of giving. So when we look at a table like this, we start asking things like: "How do the 'marrieds' differ from the 'unmarrieds' in terms of giving? Do the former give more than the latter, or vice versa? Does age affect the difference in giving between these two groups? For example, do young 'marrieds' give less than young 'unmarrieds' because they have less disposable income? But does that pattern change as people get older and their kids leave the nest?"

So summarizing a variable allows us to:

- See the variable more as a whole than as a mass of data,

- Uncover important facts about the variable, and

- Raise important questions about the relationship of the variable with other variables.

What are some good ways to summarize variables? This is an area where most statistics textbooks start confusing students and ultimately turn them off to the whole topic of statistics. For example, if you took a stats course in college or grad school, you undoubtedly had terms like these thrown at you:

- measures of central tendency

- measures of dispersion

- variance

- standard deviation

- interquartile range

- histogram

- frequency polygon

Each of these terms refers to a way of summarizing variables. And each, if you want to get into statistics in depth, is worth knowing about and studying. In fact, they're very interesting. But most peoples' eyes start glazing over at the bare mention of these terms.

So exactly how much do you really need to know about summarizing variables, for your purposes? As far as we're concerned, if you can make a table or chart that shows the percentage distribution of a variable and a vice president can understand it, then you know how to summarize a variable.

We're only half-joking about the vice president. Truth is, a lot of them tend to be number-phobic or impatient with numbers or both. And the vice president who's going to look over your results wants to understand the point of what you're trying to say, not the details of how you developed your point. So let's say you construct a table or a chart that shows a percentage distribution of a variable in your database, and you show that table to a vice president. If he or she looks interested or even intrigued (rather than looking confused or bored), you've probably found the right approach to summarizing variables.

Now let's talk about how to make a percentage distribution for a variable. We'll start with how to do it for categorical variables, because that's pretty easy. Then we'll move on to quantitative and hybrid variables, where making percentage distributions is a little more complicated—but only a little.

We've already seen an example of a percentage distribution for a categorical variable. That's Table 5.2 above, for Marital Status. Actually, this is a table for both a frequency distribution and a percentage distribution. It shows the frequency (that is, the number, or "count") of records that fall into each category of the variable as well as the percentage of records that fall into each category. Figure 5.1 shows how the percentage distribution would look in chart form.

As you can see, making up a percentage distribution for a categorical variable is pretty straightforward. All you do is ask your software to count up the number of records in each category and convert those numbers to percentages. (The percentage, if you don't remember your school math, being the count divided by the total number of records, multiplied by 100.) Then you construct either a table or a chart to display the percentages.

Now for making a percentage distribution for a quantitative variable. This is a little more complicated than making one for a categorical variable, only because a quantitative variable usually has so many categories. To explore this,

FIGURE 5.1 Percentage Distribution for MARITAL_STATUS

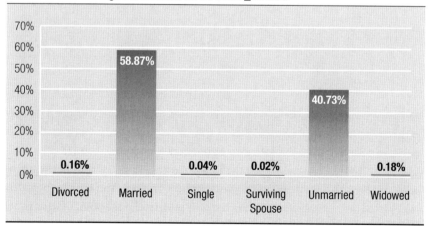

let's start with a quantitative variable that does not have a lot of categories, such as NUM_CHILDREN:

NUM_CHILDREN
1
2
2
5
3

You'll remember that NUM_CHILDREN is a hybrid variable because all the blank entries will have to be changed to something non-numeric such as the text string "Blank." But if you look at Table 5.3 and Figure 5.2, you can see there are simply not that many categories—nine in total including the blank category. That's not so many categories that we can't get a pretty good "feel" for the variable in a matter of a few seconds. Most records (almost two-thirds) fall in the "blank" category; almost all the rest represent people who have 1 to 4 kids listed in the database, and fewer than 1.5% of the records have 5 or more kids listed. In this case, the number of categories is relatively easy to present in a chart, as we see in Figure 5.2.

TABLE 5.3 Percentages and Distribution of NUM_CHILDREN

# OF CHILDREN	COUNT	%
1	423	8.46
2	797	15.94
3	333	6.66
4	121	2.42
5	41	0.82
6	13	0.26
7	2	0.04
8	1	0.02
Blank	3,269	65.38
Total	**5,000**	**100.00**

FIGURE 5.2 Percentage Distribution for NUM_CHILDREN

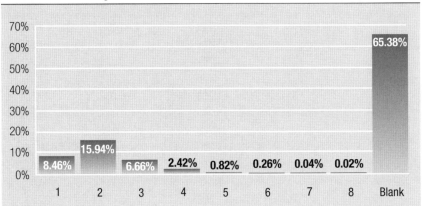

But what happens when we have a variable such as TOTAL_AMT, which lists the total dollars each individual has given the institution since that person's record has been in the database?

TOTAL_AMT
4,565.00
1,284.00
5.00
918.34
595.00
3,490.00
0.00
1,130.00
64,170.00

Now we've got a problem, because this one has 878 categories, ranging from $0 given to more than $1,000,000 given. Obviously we wouldn't consider making a table or chart with well over 800 categories. So what do we do? One solution would be to divide the variable up into a few chunks that make it easier to get our arms around it. Since about a third (34.76% to be exact) of the records in our development sample have given nothing at all to the university, one thing we could do is divide TOTAL_AMT roughly into thirds—that is, the bottom third, middle third, and top third of givers.

To do that we'll need a little help. One of the nice things about statistical software packages such as Data Desk is that they will quickly display the percentage distribution for a quantitative variable no matter how many categories it has. For

TABLE 5.4 Percentage Distribution for a Quantitative Variable

TOTAL $ GIVEN	COUNT	CUMULATIVE COUNT	%	CUMULATIVE %
0	1,738	1,738	34.76	34.76
1	8	1,746	0.16	34.92
2	1	1,747	0.02	34.94
3	1	1,748	0.02	34.96
5	35	1,783	0.70	35.66
6	2	1,785	0.04	35.70
9	1	1,786	0.02	35.72
10	54	1,840	1.08	36.80
11	1	1,841	0.02	36.82
14	1	1,842	0.02	36.84
15	24	1,866	0.48	37.32

example, what you see in Table 5.4 is a small, beginning portion of a very long table that Data Desk kicked out.

Let us explain it:

- The first column, TOTAL $ GIVEN, lists the individual total dollar amounts given to the university for all records in this sample.

- The column COUNT lists the number of people in the sample who have given that particular amount. For example, 1,738 people in this sample have given a total of zero dollars; eight people have given a total of $1 (we're not kidding); one person has given $2; and so on.

- The column CUMULATIVE COUNT lists the total number of people in that sample who have given up to a certain amount. For example, 1,866 people in this sample have given up to $15 (total) to the university.

- The fourth column, labeled "%," lists the percentage of people in this sample who have given a particular amount. For example, the 1,738 people who have given zero dollars constitute 34.76% of the total sample of 5,000 people.

- And, finally, the last column, CUMULATIVE %, lists the total percentage of people in the sample who have given up to a certain amount. For example, 37.32% of the people in this sample have given up to $15 (total) to the university.

We want to divide TOTAL_AMT into thirds. We know the bottom third is going to be people who've given $0 to the university. (Actually, since they constitute 34.76% of the sample, they make up a bit more than a third, but that's fine.)

How about the middle third? Much farther down on this long table, Data Desk tells us that 66.84% of the people in this sample have given a total of up to $250. So we know our middle third consists of people who have given more than $0 (that's our bottom third) and less than $251. In other words, our middle third consists of people who have given anywhere from $1 to $250 to the university.

And our top third? That's anyone who's given $251 or more to the university.

Table 5.5 shows how these "thirds" look in table form. Figure 5.3 shows how they look in chart form.

You know enough right now to adequately summarize any variable—categorical, quantitative, or hybrid. But there are two other measurements we can't ignore. One is called the "mean," and the other is called the "median." If you've taken any kind of a stats course, you undoubtedly recognize both terms. You may even be asking, "Ah … what about the 'mode'? Doesn't that belong in there, too?"

Let's dispense with the "mode." It just means the most frequently occurring category in any variable. You see the mode referred to all the time in statistics

TABLE 5.5 "Thirds" in Table Form

GIVING CATEGORY	COUNT	%
Bottom third ($0)	1,738	34.76
Middle third ($1–$250)	1,604	32.08
Top third ($251 or more)	1,658	33.16
Total	5,000	100.00

FIGURE 5.3 Percentage of Records Falling into Three Giving Categories

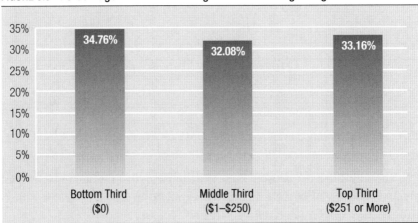

textbooks, but it rarely (very rarely) gets used in practice. But the mean and the median do get cited and used a lot with quantitative variables. So let's talk about what each term means, and then let us offer our opinion on the use of both for the kind of practical data analysis we're doing here.

"**Mean**" is just the technical term for "average"—a term we hear or read about almost every day. It refers to the sum of values for a variable in a sample divided by the number of objects/records in the sample. For example, let's take the variable TOTAL_AMT for our development sample of 5,000 records. If we add up all the amounts listed in each record, we get a total of $6,922,540. If we divide that amount by 5,000 (the number of records) in the sample, we get an amount of $1,384.51. So the mean (average) total amount that each individual has given is slightly less than $1,400.

The **median** is the midpoint of a variable—that value of a variable below which 50% of the records fall and above which 50% of the records fall. For our sample here of 5,000 records, the median value is $65. That is, in this sample, half the people have given a total of less than $65, and half have given a total of more than $65.

There's an obvious question here: Why, in this sample, is there such an enormous difference between the mean and the median (about $1,400 versus $65)? The answer is that the mean is very sensitive to extreme values, which can pull it way up or down. The median, on the other hand, is not sensitive to such extreme values.

Let's take a simple example. Say we have two samples of 11 records each:

Sample A		Sample B	
RECORD	TOTAL AMOUNT	RECORD	TOTAL AMOUNT
1	0	1	0
2	0	2	0
3	50	3	50
4	50	4	50
5	75	5	75
6	100	6	100
7	125	7	125
8	150	8	150
9	150	9	150
10	200	10	200
11	200	11	2,000

The only difference between these two samples is that the amount for record #11 in sample A is 200 and the amount for record #11 in sample B is 2,000. Otherwise, the two samples are exactly the same.

If we compute the median for both samples, what value do we get? (Remember the median is the midpoint of a variable—that value below which 50% of the records fall and above which 50% of the records fall.) It's 100, because in both samples five records fall below 100 and five records fall above 100.

But what about the means for the two samples? If we add up all the amounts for each record in sample A, we get 1,100; dividing that amount by 11, we get a mean of 100. But if we do the same arithmetic for sample B? We get a total of 2,900 and a mean of 263.64. Why? That one record (#11) in sample B makes all the difference. While that record has no effect on the median, it "pulls" the mean up quite a bit.

Statistical texts go into some detail on the advantages of using both these measures of what is technically referred to as "central tendency." Those details are definitely worth reading about if you have the time and inclination. But here all we have to say about the mean and the median is this: Use both of them. All statistical software packages provide both these measures (as well as a host of others) to describe and summarize quantitative variables. So take advantage of that. If the mean and median for a certain variable are very different (as with the pair of examples above), pay particular attention, because that difference means there are some very big or (possibly) very small values "pulling" or "dragging" the mean up or down.

The Basics of Analysis

Terms such as *data mining* or *analytics* can seem intimidating to the nonpractitioner. They shouldn't. The processes they refer to don't have to be complicated or difficult to understand. The case studies that follow in this book follow essentially the same few steps:

1. You gather some data that describes or measures some characteristic.
2. You compare a group of people in your sample who have that characteristic with a group that does not, in terms of a behavior you wish to predict (i.e., giving to your cause).
3. Via the comparison, you hope to discover a connection between the characteristic and the behavior.
4. Then you can use this connection (plus other, similar connections) to predict the behavior.

That all sounds a bit vague, we admit. So let's describe it in more concrete terms, starting with some really basic stuff.

The data in your database was not entered at random; there are patterns encoded there. Some are blindingly obvious. If Mr. A gave $100 last year, he will have a gift record in the database to indicate it. Mrs. B, who has never given, has no record for any year. A good database will include a lot more than just giving histories. There might also be information on who has attended events. Someone who has attended three events will have three event records, while someone who's never attended an event will have none.

Simple, right? All this basic information is collectively called "data."

We can categorize everyone in the database into simple groups, based on this data. For example, based on stored giving histories, we can assign all our constituents into two groups: "Donor" for anyone who has given at least a dollar at any time in the past, and "Non-donor" for everyone else. And based on the event attendance data we've managed to capture, we can sort everyone into "Attendee" (if they've attended at least one event) or "Non-attendee." Both of these are categorical variables, and binary ones as well.

Again, not hard to understand. This is a basic and typical activity, which we might call "preparing the data file." It's one step in the process of readying data for analysis. Someone in IT or advancement services may help you with this step. After that, you're on your own.

We picked event attendance and giving as our two types of data for this example for a reason that will become clear shortly. The next step is where things start to get interesting. We will see how these groups overlap. For example, Mr. A is a donor, but he must also belong to one of the events-related groups (Attendee or Non-attendee). The same with the non-donor Mrs. B.

For the sake of argument, let's say our database contains records for 10,000 living individuals. Of those, only 4,000 (or 40%) have ever made a gift.

	COUNT
Donor	4,000
Non-donor	6,000
	10,000

And only 2,000 people have ever attended an event.

	COUNT
Attendee	2,000
Non-attendee	8,000
	10,000

These tables are two ways to describe the very same set of 10,000 individuals. Therefore, these two variables (which we might call "Donor Status" and "Event Status") must intersect. By that we mean that any individual has to have both a Donor Status (donor/non-donor) *and* an Event Status (attendee/non-attendee).

For the moment, and for illustration only, let's assume that there is absolutely no relationship between being a donor and attending events. Regardless of whether a person is a donor or not, there is still a 50-50 chance that she's also an event attendee—it's a random toss of the coin. In other words, the two behaviors are completely unconnected. (Hint: The two behaviors are almost always connected, but pretend you don't know that! In fact, it is good analytical practice not to assume anything until you've demonstrated it to yourself. Why? Because every data set is unique.)

If attendance makes no difference with respect to donor status, we would expect to find the same proportion of donors within each group as we would within the whole sample of people—because it's just random. So if 40% of people in the sample are donors, we would expect that 40% of attendees are donors and 40% of non-attendees are donors, give or take.

	COUNT	EXPECTED NUMBER OF DONORS
Attendee	2,000	$2,000 \times 40\% = \quad 800$
Non-attendee	8,000	$8,000 \times 40\% = 3,200$
	10,000	4,000

We can test whether our assumption of "no connection" is correct or not, because we have the data. What are the **actual** numbers of donors in each of the two groups, Attendee and Non-attendee?

	COUNT	EXPECTED NUMBER OF DONORS	ACTUAL NUMBER OF DONORS
Attendee	2,000	800	1,200
Non-attendee	8,000	3,200	2,800
	10,000	4,000	4,000

Hmm, that's interesting. There is a big difference between what we expected to see (based on the assumption of no connection between event attendance and giving) and what we discover when we count the actual number of donors in each group. More attendees than we expected are donors, and more non-attendees than we expected are *non*-donors.

To make the difference clearer, let's drop the "expected" column and calculate a percentage for the proportion of each group that consists of donors.

	COUNT	ACTUAL NUMBER OF DONORS	PERCENTAGE WHO ARE DONORS
Attendee	2,000	1,200	60%
Non-attendee	8,000	2,800	35%
	10,000	4,000	

What have we learned here? Simply this: That for this data set, a person who has attended an event is almost twice as likely to be a donor than is a person who has never attended an event—60% versus 35%. Figure 5.4 shows the same thing as the table.

Now we know our original assumption of complete randomness was wrong, because our actual results differ so markedly from what we expected. How much of a difference would we need to see between "expected" and "actual" to know that there is a connection? When the difference isn't obvious at a glance, we need to use a statistical test of significance. Suffice to say here that the connection illustrated above is highly significant.

In this example, we've looked at the state of being a donor as a binary condition—one has either been a donor or has not been a donor. In the simple data file we built earlier on, we knew who was a donor and who wasn't by looking at the variable TOTAL_AMT. This variable contains a lot more information than just the fact of being or not being a donor—it tells us exactly how much they've given. Because it's a quantitative variable, our stats software is able to compute statistics on it such as average amount given and median amount given. We can look at

FIGURE 5.4 Percentage of Donors by Event Status

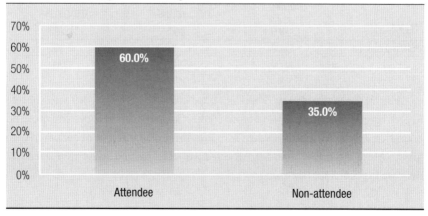

how average and median giving compare between the two groups, Attendee and Non-attendee. See Figure 5.5.

Clearly there's a huge difference: Event attendees have average giving that is much higher. But possibly there are one or two major gift donors in the Yes group, whose million-dollar gifts are distorting the average. Therefore, we need to compare medians as well. See Figure 5.6.

Fewer than half of those in the Non-attendee group have given anything to the school, while the middle value for Attendees is $125. When your comparisons of both the averages and the medians agree like this, you can be assured that you've discovered a powerful association.

There is yet another way to explore the association. Earlier on, in our explanation about how to summarize variables, we demonstrated how you might split

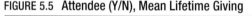

FIGURE 5.5 Attendee (Y/N), Mean Lifetime Giving

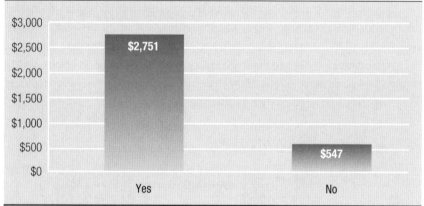

FIGURE 5.6 Attendee (Y/N), Median Lifetime Giving

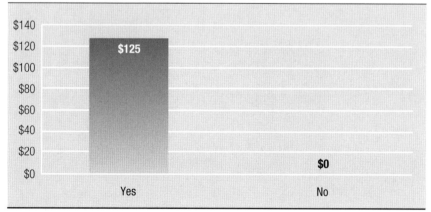

your data file into roughly equal thirds, based on total giving, the bottom third being non-donors and the other two thirds split between lower-end donors and higher-end donors—the dividing line being the median amount given for all donors in the file, which in our example was about $250. For this example, let's say the breakdowns are the same—that is, half of donors gave less than $250, and half gave $250 or more.

This is exactly what we've done in Figure 5.7, only now we are comparing how non-attendees break down by giving level, in comparison to how attendees break down by giving level. In this view, we are primarily interested in the extremes: who gives at the high end ($250+) and who doesn't give at all. We can ignore the middle zone, the donors who give between $1 and $249.

More than twice as many attendees (42.5%) have giving in the high range as non-attendees. And attendees are half as likely as non-attendees to have given nothing. Yet more evidence that event attendance and giving go hand-in-hand.

The process of comparing two variables in this example is typical of what we call *data analysis*. When we observe a connection such as this between two variables, we say that there is an association between them, or that they are *correlated*: Event attendance is associated with giving, or event attendance is correlated with giving. As you advance in your knowledge of data mining, you will encounter more sophisticated methods for measuring the degree of correlation between

FIGURE 5.7 Attendee (Y/N), by Giving Levels

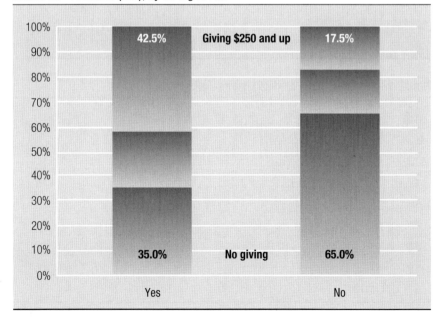

variables. For now, though, it's enough to know that the concept of correlation is at the heart of data mining.

Now we know that giving and event attendance go hand-in-hand (more often than not). We've learned something about our data. That's not enough, though. We need to *apply* that knowledge. The data we've just looked at suggests two perfect applications: Event attendance can be used to predict who is most likely to give a gift, and giving can be used to predict who is most likely to attend an event.

Let's say we have two non-donors: Mrs. B, whom we've already met, and a new person, Ms. C. Both of these women are records in a huge data file of non-donors who might be mailed as part of an annual fund appeal, in hopes of acquiring some portion of them as new donors. Unfortunately, we have only enough room in the budget to send mail to half the group. We need a way to whittle down that list.

According to our data, Mrs. B has never attended an event. Ms. C, however, came to campus for a reunion a couple of years ago. All other things being equal, which woman is more likely to be acquired as a new donor? If you said Ms. C, you're right! A fundraiser working with this data set knows that in order to narrow the field to the non-donors most likely to be converted, better results will come from mailing event attendees than from mailing non-attendees or any random selection of non-donors.

(Conversely, because the correlation is reciprocal, if we needed to narrow down a list of event invitees for an expensive mailing, we will realize better response by excluding non-donors from the mailing.)

How sure are we that Ms. C will actually give? Well, here's another important point about data mining: We can never be certain. Using the language of

We can also state the reverse: Giving is correlated with event attendance. The relationship is reciprocal. This is an important point, because sometimes when you tell someone that some behavior is correlated with giving, they assume you mean that the behavior *causes* giving. We are not making a statement about causation. Event attendance *might* cause giving (or even vice versa), but we don't know that. We are only saying that, for this population, the two behaviors tend to coincide. Figuring out what "causes" giving or event attendance, or how those behaviors may be influenced, is a far more complex and slippery concept than what we are talking about. Just to be clear, our concern is **predicting** human behavior, which is a lot easier than delving into its causes! What we do may seem scientific, but it is definitely an applied science, focused on practical, everyday outcomes.

probability, all we can say is that Ms. C is almost twice as likely to give as Mrs. B, all other things being equal. We can very easily be wrong about Mrs. B and Ms. C as individuals, but over the whole population our observation can be expected to hold roughly true.

Notice that we've been careful to say "all other things being equal." In practice, all other things are never equal. That's why if we were attempting to predict who will give, we would look at many other variables besides event attendance. Other behaviors such as whether or not the person has provided contact information (email, business phone, etc.) or demographic factors (age, marital status, etc.) may also be associated with giving. Each one would have to be tested. If a variable proves helpful in our quest of the elusive donor, then it might get added to what is called a *predictive model*—an assembly of all the variables that are associated with the state of being a donor, each variable weighted according to its relative strength of association with the desired outcome, in order to calculate a *score* for each individual—a relative measure of likelihood to give.

With every meaningful variable we add, our models and scores should become more and more reliable. But again, we will never have certainty, because our knowledge is imperfect. Our database contains only so much information about our constituents, and many factors related to giving are either not present (such as household income), or are not well-captured, or are too complex to grasp, or were not measurable to begin with.

In fact, nothing is certain when it comes to predicting human behavior. People are complicated, and they get to choose what to do at any given moment. But people's behavior is not random; it follows patterns. Some of those patterns are present in our databases, and if we are good at identifying them, we can make good guesses

The terms *data mining* and *predictive modeling* are often used interchangeably, but not because they mean exactly the same thing. There are plenty of definitions available for both terms, but data mining is any activity that involves exploring large data sets for patterns or to answer specific questions (which may or may not have anything to do with predicting behavior).

Data mining might also be the right term to describe the exploration of variables for correlation with giving, which naturally shades into the actual creation of predictive models for giving. Predictive modeling itself, though, is the creation of formulas that produce scores for each constituent in a database for the purpose of predicting that constituent's probability of engaging in a certain behavior (e.g., giving to the annual fund).

about which people to approach, which people to invite, which people to recruit. That whole process is called *predictive modeling*, or, simply, *data mining*.

Data Mining, and Not Data Mining

We can hear some of you saying it already: "Hey, Peter and Kevin are saying that event attendance is predictive of giving. So all we have to do is dig through our database for all past event attendees and ask them for a gift."

True, in study after study, school after school, event attendance has been a steady predictor of giving. So have other typical variables: marital status is "married," the alum participated in a survey, and so on and so forth. But that doesn't prove anything about *your* data. If you whip up a set of scores based on the **assumption** that these and other variables are predictive, you might have some success, because in fact many of them probably are. But you are not doing data mining, properly speaking.

The missing element is that you've failed to test in the environment of your own data. For example, the presence of an email address might be predictive in one data set, but not at all in another. And for any variable, the strength of association will differ from data set to data set—from one school to another school.

In the same vein, we have concerns about people placing a lot of faith in the use of RFM scores. RFM stands for Recency, Frequency, and Monetary value. There are various ways to calculate RFM scores, but the general idea is that a donor who has given very recently, has a history of frequent giving, and has given relatively large gifts will earn a top-level RFM score, which suggests that she is most likely to give again, or increase the size of her gift.

RFM has been used for many decades by direct marketers in the for-profit sector as a measure of customer value. It can be highly useful for fundraising as well, but it has severe limitations that make it inferior to proper predictive modeling. For example, RFM does not take elements of affinity into account (such as volunteering or attending events). Because it's purely transactional in nature, RFM provides useful information only about existing donors, but it provides no insight into which non-donors are likely to be converted.

It also can't tell you which lapsed donors are most likely to be reactivated, or which donors are most likely to be upgraded to higher levels of giving. In the eyes of RFM, one person who gave $50 last year is exactly the same as any other person who gave $50 last year. They're not.

RFM has its applications, but don't let anyone tell you that pure donor transaction data is all you need. Total reliance on giving history to inform strategy ignores the trove of other variables in your database, which is a huge waste.

When you apply an assumption to the data, the data is mute and simply yields to your manipulations. If you only manipulate the data, it's not data mining. If you ask questions of the data and let it speak for itself—and if you learn something you didn't know before—then you can call it data mining. You have discovered a pattern that you can put to practical use.

All of the studies in this book follow the same few essentials we've outlined so far:

1. We formulate a question that we think can lead to a useful result. ("Is event attendance related to giving?")

2. Some relevant data is collected, so that we can categorize the subjects of our analysis, or assign some value to the characteristic we are measuring. (Donors vs. Non-donors, Attendees vs. Non-attendees— OR, dollars given, number of events attended.)

3. Comparisons are made between groups by looking at proportions, as we did in our example, or by using some other type of comparison. The result of the comparison informs us whether there is an association between a variable and a behavior of interest (e.g., giving).

chapter 6

Analytics for Other Advancement Functions

ata-driven decision-making isn't just for fundraisers. Your staff members in alumni relations can also gain useful insights via data mining. We've created propensity models for likelihood to attend events (used for slimming down invitation mailings) and likelihood to volunteer (to help decide whom to approach). There's no reason other models could not be created—likelihood to respond to affinity program promotions such as alumni credit cards or insurance, for example.

In chapter 5, we showed how being an event attendee could be linked to a higher likelihood of being a donor. Such a linkage is called an association, or correlation. (The term *correlation* has a more precise definition in statistics, but we've used it in this book in a more approximate sense.) That linkage is reciprocal: Event attendance is linked to giving, and giving is equally linked to event attendance. We can say this because we are not claiming that one activity *causes* the other. We're only saying that the behaviors tend to coincide in the same individual. (This is what is meant by the common saying "Correlation is not causation.") So if event attendance can be used to predict who will give, because the two tend to be found together, then giving can be used to predict who will attend events.

As we said in chapter 5, a good database will include a lot more than just giving histories. There might also be information on who has attended events. We can categorize everyone in the database into simple groups, based on this data. Every record can be identified as either "Donor" or "Non-donor," and the same records can also be identified as either "Attendee" (if the person has come to at least one event) or "Non-attendee." Every person in the database will have a code for both conditions: giving and attending. In chapter 5, we looked at how those two behaviors overlapped in a hypothetical data set.

That data set contained 10,000 records, each one an individual living alum. Forty percent of the sample had some giving to the university; those 4,000 records were flagged "Donor," and the rest "Non-donor." Our example highlighted an interesting and useful relationship with event attendance. To summarize:

- 60% of alumni who have attended at least one event are donors.

- Only 35% of alumni who have *never* attended an event are donors.

In other words, alumni who have attended events are twice as likely to be donors as alumni who haven't attended events. Given the large size of our data set, we can be confident this is not a random effect: There is a strong association between event attendance and giving. We also showed that there is a strong association (correlation) between event attendance and the *lifetime amount* given. For our sample, more than twice as many event attendees had giving in the top range of total giving ($250 and up) as the non-attendees.

Having established that giving and event attendance go hand-in-hand in a given data set, you can then use one behavior to predict the other. Imagine a fundraiser working on the annual fund who needs to slim down her donor acquisition mailing. Lacking any other information to go on, she knows she'll have better luck converting non-donors who have some history of event attendance than she will with non-attendee non-donors or with any random selection of non-donors.

Now imagine an alumni officer who needs to slim down a mailing for an event invitation. There isn't enough money available to mail everyone, nor time enough to phone everyone. For the best return on investment, he needs to guess who is most likely to attend and focus on them. Naturally he'll want to invite everyone who has attended an event in that city before. Let's imagine, however, that very few alumni in this particular city have any history of event attendance. He's flying blind. Can he make use of the same information that guided his fundraiser colleague? Yes, he can.

How so? Recall that we said correlation is a reciprocal relationship. Saying "A is correlated with B" is precisely the same thing as saying "B is correlated with A." Event attenders are more likely to be donors; therefore, donors are more likely to attend events. Lacking any other information, this alumni officer can at least ensure that all donors make the invite list. Even better, a predictive model that combines donor status with other variables will be helpful in narrowing down on the "best bets" for this mailing. Many of the variables that are significant predictors of giving will also figure prominently in predicting event attendance:

presence of contact information, participation in a survey, a record of student involvement, volunteering, and so on.

Any variable that is normally a predictor could potentially be turned into something you might want to try to predict. Taken to an extreme, you might even try to predict whether someone in your database is probably male or probably female, based on other variables. Whether doing so is useful or not depends on the context. We think it's wisest if you stick to identifying behaviors, especially ones that are desirable: responding, purchasing, attending, volunteering, mentoring, and giving.

Now let's back up a few steps. Our ability to predict a behavior is based entirely on having clear historical examples of that exact activity stored in the database. Are your volunteers coded as such in the database? If not, you won't be able to determine the characteristics of a volunteer, and you won't be able to find other people in your database who share that set of characteristics—and who, although they aren't volunteers now, are statistically more likely to respond to your approach than someone picked at random or identified by some other haphazard way. The same goes for your would-be mentors, event attendees, and, yes, your donors.

Your institution almost certainly does a good job tracking who's been a donor, when they gave and how much—no issue there. Fewer institutions are as diligent about capturing and storing volunteer and other alumni engagement-related data, unfortunately. You may already be pleading with your alumni relations colleagues to ensure this data gets in. Perhaps they do not find data mining for fundraising a compelling enough reason to comply. (We will pass on making a judgment about whether they are suited for their jobs in that case.) Well, here are a few reasons they might readily grasp:

- Pre-entering RSVPs, if your database allows it, enables an efficient way of producing event bios (what in some shops are called "blurbs"), by pulling all the relevant data from your database for the IDs that have an RSVP in their record for the event, such as total giving, spouse name, class year, degree, etc.

- Statistics for attendance at key annual events are much more easily generated when the data is stored in the database. Not just attendee counts, but breakdowns by class year, milestone reunion year, giving, and so on.

- If your school is serious about performance management, alumni staff performance metrics will have to include event stats, and those reports have to be pulled from the database.

- It's easy to pull a mailing list of event attendees, for post-event surveying.

- Event attendance history is a useful piece of information to incorporate in major-gift prospect profiles. Having it in one place (ideally as part of a report) will make it easier to retrieve quickly.

None of these reasons has anything to do with predictive modeling. They're all very practical but short-term uses of data. The ultimate, long-term value of this data is the insight it gives into which of your alumni are engaged. Surely some of your colleagues in alumni relations would "get it" if they were shown how data mining could save them money on their event mailings, increase their success with recruiting volunteers and mentors, and help them identify their most-engaged alumni.

Now that we mention alumni engagement, let us close now with a word or two on that subject. We encounter a lot of misunderstanding about alumni engagement. A common misconception is that an alum's level of engagement is best determined by asking him what he thinks: The ones who respond positively are highly engaged, and the ones who complain bitterly are not engaged. This is the wisdom of surveying and focus groups, and whatever the merits of either of those tools (and they certainly do have merits when employed properly), such a conclusion is probably mistaken.

The constituents in your database who are not engaged are not the ones who write nasty letters. They're not the ones who give you a big thumbs-down on your survey. They're not the ones who criticize the food at your gala dinner. They're not the ones who tell your phone campaign callers never to call again. Nope. Your truly non-engaged constituents are the ones you never hear from. They are the ones who chuck out your mailings unopened. The ones who ignore the invitation to participate in a survey. The ones who have never attended an event. The ones who never answer the phone.

If your school or organization is typical, a good-sized portion of your database falls into this non-engaged category. There's money in identifying who is truly not engaged and therefore not worth wasting resources on. The ones who are moved to criticize you, the ones who have opinions about you, the ones who want to be contacted only a certain way—they're engaged.

The future belongs to those who can tell the difference.

part 3

CASE STUDIES IN DATA ANALYSIS

Please Try This at Home

OVER THE YEARS, Peter, Kevin, and John Sammis have cooper-ated to produce a lot of discussion papers for publication online, via either the CASE website or the CoolData blog. These papers have ranged over a wide array of topics at the intersection of higher education advancement and the data that institutions have at their disposal. Mostly they are about things that Peter and John have discovered through the process of working with client schools' data—sometimes finding things they weren't looking for! We've always followed our nose—whatever we've found most fascinating *and* potentially useful—and sometimes that has led us into areas where we suspect few have ventured before.

As a result, what we've produced has usually been more of an essay (as in the French origin of the word, *essayer,* meaning "to try" or "to attempt") rather than a thoroughgoing analysis of the sort you'd find in a peer-reviewed academic journal. The intent is to generate discussion (even disagreement, if it comes to that) and to spark new ideas in the heads of readers keen to make discoveries in their own data. That's why we have always invited readers to share their comments, and it's been gratifying to see how our hopes for our work have been fulfilled.

On the other hand, occasionally there will be the reader who says that our paper is "interesting, but ..." She wants to know if we've tried doing *this*, or why didn't we take *that* into account. The questions and suggestions are not unreasonable, and if we had any intention of redoing the analysis, we'd probably find them really helpful.

But that's not the point. In raising this or that related issue, or suggesting alternate approaches for us, our online reviewers sometimes get too hung up on the details instead of grasping the central idea of the paper and taking that as a jumping-off point. Not to seem ungrateful to readers who have taken the time to offer their thoughtful comments, but we feel they're often missing a key message that is even more important than any individual paper: We expect readers (regardless of skill level) to grab hold of their own data and make their own "essay." We'd love to see more people attempting to replicate our studies. And if there are readers who are intelligent and thorough enough to be thinking of additional factors or approaches to consider, then we have even greater expectations of *them*.

Some people who regard the work as "interesting" but not something they see as intended to spur them to action may be under the impression that what we're doing is conducting research to unearth trends in donor behavior that apply universally, as if we were searching for a grand theory, doing work that doesn't really apply to the day-to-day practitioner. Nothing could be more wrong. When we desire that others replicate our studies, we aren't necessarily looking for people to replicate our *results*. We just want them to try to do the darn study. These studies are usually conducted on data from one school at a time, and rarely more than three or four schools. We are not out to prove any general theories. We can't. Our findings might apply to your institution's data, and they might not. It's up for YOU to figure that out. And if you find that rather challenging, along with being interesting, then so much the better. Because there really is no better way to learn.

Our feeling is that if what we're putting out there is just "interesting," then we've done only half a job. You, the person reading this book, probably have access to data that you can analyze just as well as we can. So the case studies that follow are intended to be more than just interesting—they're intended to be actionable.

chapter 7

The Annual Fund
Focusing Limited Resources

nnual fund professionals spend a lot of time refining the precise details of their approach to prospective donors: whether to use postage-paid return envelopes or not, whether to use a hand-applied first class stamp or go with metered mail, whether a student or Dean So-and-So should sign the appeal letter, whether each renewal donor will get five or seven or 10 call attempts from the phone campaign—and many other, similar nuances that are the subject of the bulk of discussions on listservs that deal with annual fund.

Sometimes these nuances make a difference in success rates, sometimes they don't. The better annual fund programs perform random tests to determine which messages or approaches work best. But it's our assertion that most of this stuff matters a lot less than one key thing: whether we are doing a good job identifying who likes us. The emotions, opinions, and feelings that would-be donors have when they think of our institution, organization, or cause trump just about everything else.

Yes, there are right and wrong ways to communicate with donors and would-be donors, but it seems unlikely that tinkering with our letterhead, our brand, or our scripts has a great deal of influence over the decision of whether or not to give when compared with the feelings and emotions of our constituents. Alas, fundraisers have a hard time distinguishing between meaningful practices and mere refinements. We keep changing the color of our sails in hopes the ship will go faster.

We need to get a whole lot better at identifying who likes us, and pay attention to them. If they like us a lot, we need to ask them, thank them, upgrade them, stay with them on the journey—as all our fundraising experience and human instincts guide us to do. If they like us a little, perhaps we can do something to engage them. If they are indifferent, we must simply walk away.

That does not mean we should pay attention only to donors: There are all kinds of people who haven't given, but will someday. They reveal their affinity in ways that most fundraisers don't take into account. And among donors, these clues regarding affinity help define the donor who is ready to give much more, or remain loyal for a lifetime, or even leave a bequest. Identifying "who likes us," regardless of whether they've given or not, separating them from the rest of the crowd for special attention—this is what predictive modeling can do for you.

case study one   ACQUIRING NEW ALUMNI DONORS

It's a truism: The people who have already given, and given recently, are the most likely to give this year. Renewing and upgrading existing donors is a key concern in annual fund efforts. But it's far from the whole picture. Not every donor can be relied on to continue giving year after year; in fact, many never make it to their second gift. The fact of donor attrition forces fundraisers to also consider how to attract new donors to the fold, in order to ensure the long-term health of the program.

Many institutions and nonprofits invest heavily in acquiring new donors. Calling and mailing to never-donors yields a return on investment that may be nonexistent in the short term and difficult to quantify in the (future) long term. Donor acquisition is hard. If you don't believe that, talk to anyone who runs the annual fund for a large university. Ask them about their success rates with calling and mailing to never-givers. They will emit sighs of frustration and exasperation. They will tell you about the depressing pledge rates from the thousands and thousands of letters and postcards they send out. They will tell you about the enervating effect of wrong numbers and hang-ups on their student callers.

Yet it must be done. ROI is important, but if you write off whole segments based only on ROI in the current year, ignoring long-term value, your pool of donors will shrink through attrition. Broadening the base of new donors costs money—an investment we hope to recoup with interest when new donors renew in future years. Some recent research on donor psychology suggests that giving can be habitual, and a number of fundraising experts have said that we should think about "lifetime value" rather than short-term returns when deciding continuing expensive acquisition efforts is worthwhile.

Unfortunately, estimating lifetime value—the sum of all gifts each donor will make over the course of their life—is complicated and prone to error. A better beginning point might be to determine who among our constituents is most likely to convert. We won't know their long-term value to our program, but at least in the short term we will know that we aren't wasting money chasing people who will *not* convert.

RFM won't help. (RFM stands for "**R**ecency of Giving," "**F**requency of Giving," and "**M**onetary Value of Giving." It's a term that came out of the private sector world of direct marketing more than 40 years ago.) Applying that concept to our world of higher education advancement, you would call and mail to alums who've given recently, often, and a lot. Great idea. But if we're focused on non-donors ... call it a hunch ... that's probably not going to work out too well.

Not long ago, John Sammis helped us with a study of which alumni of higher-education institutions are most likely to make a first gift. In studying the data from hundreds of clients, sadly, the bottom line is this: In North America the lifetime hard credit alumni participation of at least half of our higher education institutions is less than 50%. If you look at only private institutions, the view is better. Public institutions? Better to not even peek out the window.*

We don't have all the answers on this complex issue. In fact, we believe that institutional leadership (from your president and board of trustees) is what's most important in getting more alums involved in giving. Data-driven decision-making is only part of the solution. However, after all that, we have had some success with building predictive models for donor acquisition. They're not great models, but, as John likes to say, "They're a heck of a lot better than throwing darts."

We are going to show you some very limited data from three schools—data that may shed just a little light on which of your non-giving alums are going to be a bit easier than others to attract into the giving fold. Again, nothing we show you here is cause for jumping up and down and dancing on the table. Far from it. But we do think it's intriguing and worth sharing with colleagues and supervisors. And at the end, we'll show you a makeshift score that you might test at your own school.

As we said, the data came from three schools: one a private institution in the U.S. Northeast, the other two public institutions in the U.S. Southeast—one medium size, the other quite small. The most important aspect of the data we got from each school is lifetime giving (for the exact same group of alums) collected at two points in time. With one school (A), the time interval we looked at stretched out over five years. For the other two (B and C), the interval was just a year. However, with all three schools we were able to clearly identify alumni who had converted from non-donor to donor status over the time interval.

We collected a lot of other information from each school, but the data we'll focus on here includes:

- Preferred year of graduation
- Home Phone Listed (Yes/No)
- Business Phone Listed (Yes/No)
- Email Address Listed (Yes/No)

For some documentation you can read "Benchmarking Lifetime Giving in Higher Education" (www.case.org/Documents/CURRENTS/July09/WylieSammisBenchmarkPaper.pdf).

The result that we paid most attention to in this study is that a greater percentage of new donors came from the ranks of recent grads than from "older" grads. To arrive at this result we:

- Divided all alums into one of four roughly equal size groups. If you look at Figure 7.1, you'll see that these groups consisted of the oldest 25% of alums who graduated in 1976 and earlier, the next oldest 25% of alums who graduated between the years 1977 and 1990, and so on.

- For each class year quartile we computed the percentage of those alums who became new donors over the time interval we looked at.

Notice in Figure 7.1 that, as the graduation years of the alums in School A becomes more recent, their likelihood of becoming a new donor goes up. In the oldest quartile (1976 and earlier), the conversion rate is 1.2%, 1.5% for those graduating between 1977 and 1990, 3% for those graduating between 1991 and 1997, and 7.5% for alums graduating in 1998 or later. You'll see a similar (but less pronounced) pattern in Figures 7.2 and 7.3 for Schools B and C.

At this point you may be saying, "Hold on a second. There are more non-donors in the more recent class year quartiles than in the older class year quartiles, right?"

"Right."

"So maybe those conversion rates are misleading. Maybe if you just looked at the conversion rates of previous non-donors by class year quartiles, those percentages would flatten out."

FIGURE 7.1   Percentage of New Donors by Class Year Quartile for School A

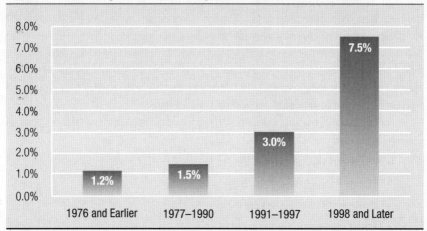

FIGURE 7.2   Percentage of New Donors by Class Year Quartile for School B

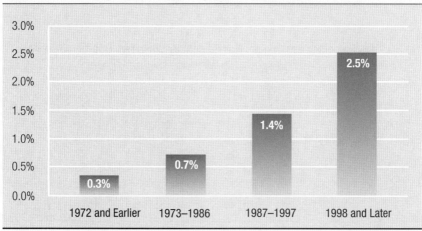

FIGURE 7.3   Percentage of New Donors by Class Year Quartile for School C

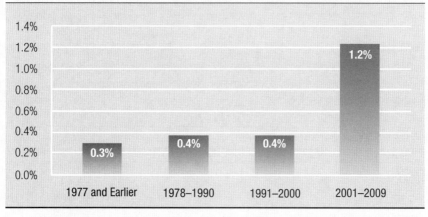

Good point. Take a look at Figures 7.1a, 7.2a, and 7.3a, which show the percentage of each age group that were non-donors.

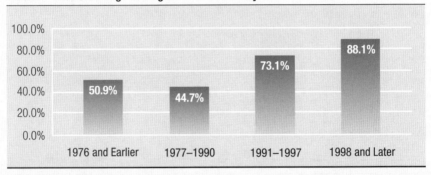

FIGURE 7.1a Percentage of Original Non-Donors by Class Year Quartile for School A

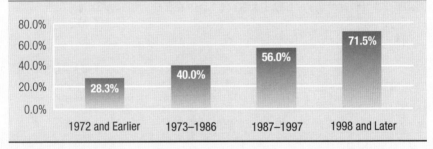

FIGURE 7.2a Percentage of Original Non-Donors by Class Year Quartile for School B

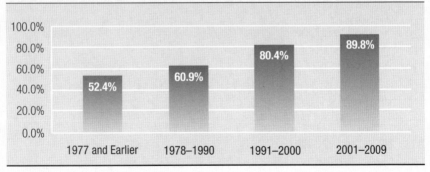

FIGURE 7.3a Percentage of Original Non-Donors by Class Year Quartile for School C

Clearly the pool of non-donors diminishes the longer alums have been out of school. So let's recompute the conversion rates for each of the three schools based solely on previous non-donors. Does that make a difference? Take a look at Figures 7.1b, 7.2b, and 7.3b.

FIGURE 7.1b   Percentage of New Donors (from Original Non-Donors)
by Class Year Quartile for School A

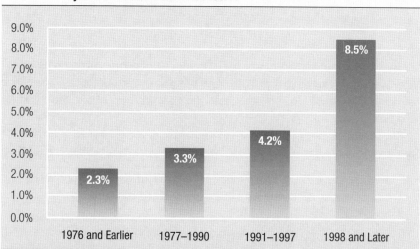

FIGURE 7.2b   Percentage of New Donors (from Original Non-Donors)
by Class Year Quartile for School B

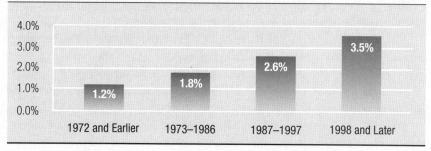

FIGURE 7.3b   Percentage of New Donors (from Original Non-Donors)
by Class Year Quartile for School C

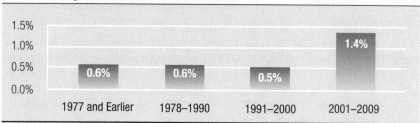

It does make some difference. But without getting any more carried away with the arithmetic here, the message is clear. Many more new donors are coming from the more recent alums than they are from the ones who graduated a good while back.

Now let's look at the three other variables we chose for this study:

- Home Phone Listed (Yes/No)
- Business Phone Listed (Yes/No)
- Email Address Listed (Yes/No)

Specifically, we wanted to know if previous non-donors with a home phone listed were more likely to convert than previous non-donors *without* a home phone listed. And we wanted to know the same thing for business phone listed and for email address listed.

The overall answer is "yes"; the detailed answers are contained in Figures 7.4 through 7.6. For the sake of clarity, let's go through Figure 7.4 together. It shows that:

- In School A, 5.8% of previous non-donors with a home phone listed converted; 3.7% without a home phone listed converted.
- In School B, 3.7% of previous non-donors with a home phone listed converted; 1.2% without a home phone listed converted.
- In School C, 1.0% of previous non-donors with a home phone listed converted; 0.4% without a home phone listed converted.

Looking at Figures 7.5 and 7.6 you can see a similar pattern of differences for whether or not a business phone or an email address was listed.

What comes across from all these figures is that the variables we've chosen to look at in this study (year of graduation, home phone, email, and business phone) don't show big differences between previous non-donors who converted and previous non-donors who did not convert. They show *small* differences. There's no getting around that.

What's encouraging (at least we think so) is that these differences are consistent across the three schools. And since the schools are quite different from one another, we expect that the same kinds of differences are likely to hold true at many other schools. Let's assume you're willing to give us the benefit of the doubt on that. Let's further assume you'd like to check out our proposition at your own school by creating a makeshift score that you might test.

Here's what we did for the data we've shown you for each of the three schools. We created four 0/1 variables for all alumni who were non-donors at the first point in time:

- Youngest Class Year Quartile. Alums who were in this group were assigned a 1; all others were assigned a 0.

FIGURE 7.4   Percentage of New Donors by Whether a Home Phone Is Listed or Not,
Across the Three Schools

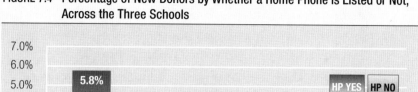

FIGURE 7.5   Percentage of New Donors by Whether or Not a Business Phone
Is Listed or Not, Across the Three Schools

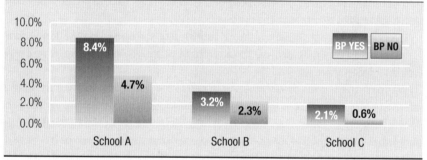

FIGURE 7.6   Percentage of New Donors by Whether an Email Address
Is Listed or Not, Across the Three Schools

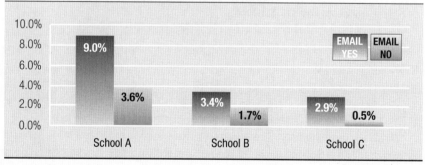

- Home Phone Listed. Alums who had a home phone listed in the database were assigned a 1; all others were assigned a 0.

- Business Phone Listed. Alums who had a business phone listed in the database were assigned a 1; all others were assigned a 0.

- Email Listed. Alums who had an email address listed in the database were assigned a 1; all others were assigned a 0.

For each alum who was a non-donor at the first point in time, we created a simple score by adding each of the above variables together. Here's the formula we used:

SCORE = Youngest Class Year Quartile (0/1) + Home Phone Listed (0/1) + Business Phone Listed (0/1) + Email Listed (0/1)

If an alumna has a score of 0, that means she was not in the Youngest Class Year Quartile, did not have a home phone listed, did not have a business phone listed and did not have an email address listed. If an alumnus has a score of 1, that means he met only one of these criteria, but not the other three. And so on up to an alum with a score of 4, who met all the criteria.

Figures 7.7 through 7.9 show the relationship of the score to new donor conversion. We'd like you to browse through them. After you do that we have a few concluding comments.

We think the figures are interesting because they show that using just a little information from an alumni database can point to folks who are far more likely to convert than other folks. Obviously, the score we created here (and suggest you try out at your own school) is very simple. Far more accurate scores can be developed using more advanced statistical techniques and the vast amount of information that's included in almost all alumni databases.

FIGURE 7.7 Percentage of Previous Non-Donors Who Became New Donors by Score Level at School A

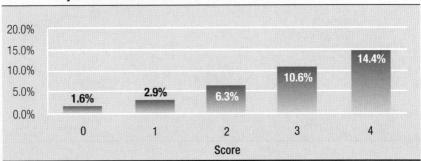

If you worked at any of these three schools and controlled the budget for donor acquisition, which group of alumni would you choose to focus on? Whom would you exclude?

Higher education fundraisers are slowly coming around to making a commitment to the use of internal alumni database information. And yet, every year, institutions of higher education waste millions of dollars on appeals (both mail and phone) to alumni who are very unlikely to ever become donors.

If this is true of data that is readily available in the database, it's even more true of data collected outside the database, via your telefund or phonathon program—the subject of our next discussion.

FIGURE 7.8   Percentage of Previous Non-Donors Who Became New Donors by Score Level at School B

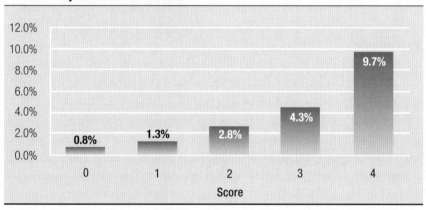

FIGURE 7.9   Percentage of Previous Non-Donors Who Became New Donors by Score Level at School C

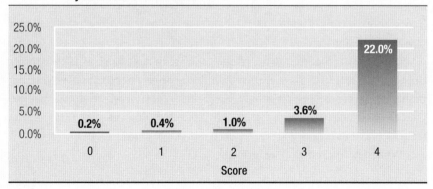

Mine Your Hidden Call Center Data

If your institution is fortunate enough to have a call center that is automated, you may be sitting on a wealth of data that never makes it into the institutional database. (Thus, "hidden.") It is frequently the case that only a few things are loaded into your institution's database from your call center: Address updates, employment updates, any requested contact restrictions, and the pledges themselves. The rest stays in the database behind the calling software. If you can get your hands on historical data from calling seasons of the recent past, you'll find all sorts of interesting bits to play around with.

With John Sammis, we have almost carved out a niche in the area of showing people how to analyze call center data for fundraising. You just won't find a lot out there on the subject. That's not to brag—we actually think it's a shame. It boggles the mind that every year college and university call centers rack up massive amounts of data on these personal points of connection with alumni and then do nothing with it.

Call center data is not just about the phonathon program. Gathered from many thousands of interactions across a broad swath of your constituency, this data can reveal propensity to give via other channels, or propensity to make a planned gift or even a major gift. But first it has to be retrieved from where it is stored. Any computerized, automated calling application relies on a back-end database. Each season, before calling begins, the prospect data (names, phone numbers, and probably some giving history) is retrieved from the institution's database and loaded into the calling database. Throughout the call season, new data is added to each prospect record: number of call attempts, the result of each call, the duration of the call in seconds, pledge data, and updates to contact information.

Some of this new information is retrieved at regular intervals (usually daily) and loaded back into the institutional database: pledges and gifts and contact information, mostly. The rest of the data stays behind and most of the time it never sees the light of day.

Prospects are loaded into the phone database in large batches that are sometimes called "projects." Usually there is only one project per term or per year, but multiple projects can be run at once. Each one is like its own separate database. One can assemble a history of contact by collecting and summarizing the data from all previous calling projects for each individual alum.

What data are you looking for?

- **ID.** Naturally, you'll need prospect IDs in order to match your data up, both across calling projects and with individuals in your database.

- **Last result code.** The last call result coded by the student caller (No Pledge, Answering Machine, etc.)

- **Number of attempts.** This is the number of times a prospect was called before you finally reached them or gave up.

- **Refusal reason.** The reason given by the prospect for not making a pledge, sometimes chosen by the phonathon employee from a drop-down menu of the most common responses. Refusal reasons are not always well-tracked, but they're potentially useful for designing strategies aimed at overcoming objections. We've observed in the past that certain refusal reasons are actually predictive of giving (by mail).

- **Talk time.** The length of the call, in seconds. People who pledge are on the phone longer, of course, but not every long call results in a pledge.

There are other important types of information—address and employment updates, method of payment, and so on—but it is likely that this data has been transferred to your database and you do not need to extract it from your phonathon database. The focus is on hidden data—the stuff that gets left behind.

That's just the beginning. You'll need to put some thought into the variables you will create. For example, should you simply add up all call attempts into a single variable called "Attempts," or should you calculate an average number of attempts, keeping in mind that some prospects were called in some projects and not others? The answer will vary depending on what you want to do with the data.

case study two   **TIME ON THE CALL**

It's a Wednesday evening and you're in the call center watching your students on the phone with alumni. Young people talking to older people who went to the same school they did. Lots of drama. Smiles. Frowns. Glee. Frustration. Side conversations between callers that you hope your alums will never overhear. Maybe you're looking forward to going home and relaxing, but you're not bored. Too much energy in the room for that.

One of the things you notice, as you so often have, is the length of the calls. Some end quickly. Some go on for a while. And some last a goodly amount of time, maybe longer than you're comfortable with. Perhaps you ask yourself, "Is all that time worth the effort in terms of getting alums to pledge and pledge a lot?"

There may not be a definitive answer to that question. However, we can offer some findings we think are intriguing. Admittedly, the data we have is from only one school. There's no way we can responsibly generalize these findings to other schools. But we want to put them out there for you to think about and (we hope) test out at your own institution.

Although this example analysis uses data from only one school, we have analyzed call data from a handful of schools, and all show similar patterns that are interesting and potentially very useful for fundraisers. As you read this, think about how you might uncover insights to aid your own institution's efforts.

We'll start by showing you the basic data we looked at, then the questions we asked ourselves as we worked through the data.

This data came from a university with about 100,000 living alumni and was collected during one fall term of calling by 26 student employees working in evening shifts of 8 to 12 people each.

In this study, we explored a tiny portion of the data that was available to us:

- The results of the last call made to 4,785 alumni: "Already Pledged," "Do Not Call," "No Pledge," "Remove from List," "Specified Pledge" (including the dollar amount), and "Unspecified Pledge."

- The time (in seconds) spent on each of these 4,785 calls.

- The amount of the last gift (if there had been one) made by the alum.

These are the basic questions we tried to answer:

- How much time was spent on these almost 5,000 calls?

- What was the relationship between time spent on these calls and dollars pledged?

- What was the relationship between time spent on these calls and pledge rate?

- What was the relationship between time spent on these calls and whether or not alumni gave more than their last gift?

Take a look at the Table 7.1, which summarizes call lengths by dividing all calls into 20 roughly equally-sized groups.

TABLE 7.1   Median, Minimum, and Maximum Seconds Devoted to 4,785 Calls Made for Pledges

TIME INTERVAL	# OF CALLS MADE	TOTAL # OF SECONDS FOR ALL CALLS	MEDIAN SECONDS PER CALL	MINIMUM SECONDS	MAXIMUM SECONDS
1	231	12,360	54	23	66
2	239	18,698	78	67	88
3	237	23,206	98	89	105
4	242	27,284	113	106	119
5	244	30,507	125	120	130
6	237	32,145	136	131	140
7	236	34,218	145	141	149
8	227	34,972	154	150	158
9	248	40,713	164	159	169
10	251	43,794	175	170	179
11	239	44,300	185	180	191
12	236	46,601	198	192	204
13	238	50,318	212	205	218
14	239	54,234	227	219	235
15	239	58,180	243	236	254
16	242	64,790	266	255	283
17	240	71,980	299	284	319
18	241	83,083	344	320	372
19	238	97,495	410	373	455
20	241	156,053	556	456	2,115

Let's start with the first column in the table, "Time Interval." Notice that there are 20 of them, and that they each contain about 5% of the calls made. If you scan over to the two columns on the right ("Minimum Seconds" and "Maximum Seconds"), here's what emerges:

- A good half (Intervals 1–10) of the calls lasted less than three minutes (179 seconds).

- 80% of the calls (Intervals 1–16) lasted less than five minutes (283 seconds).

- 5% of the calls (Interval 20) lasted somewhere between seven and a half minutes (456 seconds) on up to well over half an hour (2,115 seconds).

Data we've analyzed from other schools shows a similar pattern. Some schools seem to have longer or shorter average call lengths—chattier student callers?—but overall the differences are not huge.

What was the relationship between time spent on these calls and dollars pledged? This is where things start to get interesting. Take a look at Table 7.2 and Figure 7.10. Here's what we see:

- The big news from both the table and the chart is that, as the calls get longer, there is a substantial rise in the number of pledges made per attempt, as expressed in average dollars per call attempt. There are some blips, some ups and downs, but the trend is undeniable.

- More specifically, let's compare what came in dollar-wise from the shortest 25% of calls (Intervals 1–5) and the longest 25% of calls (Intervals 16–20). It's $3,910 versus $62,491. Any way you do the math, that's a big difference.

TABLE 7.2 Total and Mean Pledge Dollars Received by Call Time Interval

TIME INTERVAL	# OF CALLS MADE	TOTAL PLEDGE DOLLARS RECEIVED	MEDIAN PLEDGE DOLLARS RECEIVED (PER ATTEMPT)
1	231	$330	$1.43
2	239	$145	$0.61
3	237	$1,155	$4.87
4	242	$535	$2.21
5	244	$1,745	$7.15
6	237	$625	$2.64
7	236	$805	$3.41
8	227	$1,865	$8.22
9	248	$2,687	$10.83
10	251	$3,093	$12.32
11	239	$3,560	$14.90
12	236	$4,415	$18.71
13	238	$5,935	$24.94
14	239	$4,390	$18.37
15	239	$6,727	$28.15
16	242	$8,855	$36.59
17	240	$9,970	$41.54
18	241	$11,071	$45.94
19	238	$16,620	$69.83
20	241	$15,975	$66.29

FIGURE 7.10 Mean Pledge Dollars Received by Call Time Interval

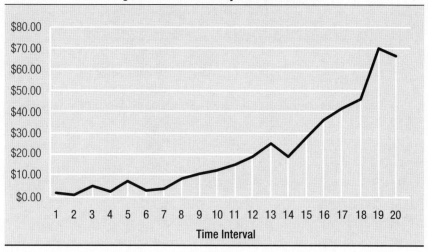

What was the relationship between time spent on these calls and pledge rate? Look at Table 7.3 and Figure 7.11.

We see the same pattern here as we did with pledge dollars received. If anything, the relationship is a bit stronger. The shortest 25% of calls (Intervals 1–5) yielded 37 pledges. The longest 25% of calls (Intervals 16–20) yielded 678 pledges. This is a big, big difference.

You might well wonder if the relationship simply means that a call that includes a pledge takes longer to complete than a call that results in "no pledge." In other words, the relationship is readily explainable and not interesting. Very well. Let's look at something else.

What was the relationship between time spent on these calls and whether or not alums *gave more than their last gift*? This may be the most interesting question of all. We all want alumni to give more this time than they gave the last time, whether we are reaching out to them by a call or a letter or a visit.

TABLE 7.3 Pledge Percentage by Call Time Interval

TIME INTERVAL	# OF CALLS MADE	TOTAL # OF PLEDGES RECEIVED	PLEDGE % FOR INTERVAL	% OF PLEDGES RECEIVED (CUMULATIVE)
1	231	2	0.90%	0.18%
2	239	3	1.30%	0.27%
3	237	11	4.60%	0.98%
4	242	6	2.50%	0.53%
5	244	19	7.80%	1.69%
6	237	14	5.90%	1.24%
7	236	13	5.50%	1.15%
8	227	24	10.60%	2.13%
9	248	32	12.90%	2.84%
10	251	33	13.10%	2.93%
11	239	46	19.20%	4.08%
12	236	45	19.10%	3.99%
13	238	61	25.60%	5.41%
14	239	57	23.80%	5.06%
15	239	83	34.70%	7.36%
16	242	103	42.60%	9.14%
17	240	111	46.30%	9.85%
18	241	134	55.60%	11.89%
19	238	161	67.60%	14.29%
20	241	169	70.10%	15.00%

FIGURE 7.11 Pledge Percentage by Call Time Interval

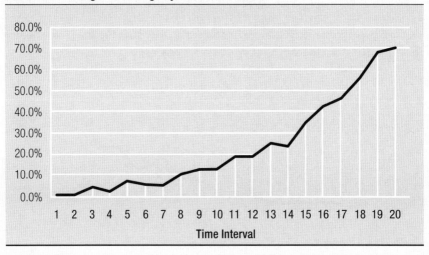

Same suggestion: Look at Table 7.4 and Figure 7.12. Then we'll tell you what we think.

TABLE 7.4   Number and Percentage of Pledges Received Greater Than Previous Pledge by Call Time Interval

TIME INTERVAL	# OF CALLS MADE	TOTAL # OF PLEDGES RECEIVED GREATER THAN PREVIOUS PLEDGE	% OF GREATER PLEDGES RECEIVED
1	231	1	0.4%
2	239	0	0.0%
3	237	2	0.8%
4	242	2	0.8%
5	244	2	0.8%
6	237	1	0.4%
7	236	4	1.7%
8	227	6	2.6%
9	248	4	1.6%
10	251	13	5.2%
11	239	16	6.7%
12	236	14	5.9%
13	238	23	9.7%
14	239	21	8.8%
15	239	33	13.8%
16	242	34	14.0%
17	240	48	20.0%
18	241	57	23.7%
19	238	51	21.4%
20	241	80	33.2%

FIGURE 7.12   Percentage of Pledges Received Greater Than Previous Pledge by Call Time Interval

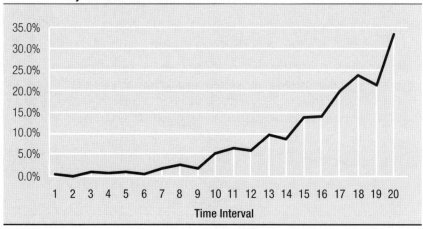

No doubt about it. The longer the call lasted, the more likely alums were to give more this time than they had the last time.

What does all this mean? Before we answer that question, we should warn you not to fall into the trap of making a causal inference. For example, we can't conclude that encouraging callers to spend more time on the phone with alums who pick up the phone is going to increase participation and revenue. Spending more time on the phone with these folks may be a cause of increased giving, or it may not.

Why do we say that? Because time spent on the phone may not be the causal factor at work here. What may be making the difference are factors *related* to how much time the caller spends on the phone with the alum. It could be that warmer and chattier callers are better at raising money with alums who are also warm and chatty—and it's that combination of traits that leads to longer calls, and it's the chemistry between the two people that produces the pledge. Or the alum has fond memories of university and enjoys speaking with students, along with giving generously. We don't know.

Although we cannot jump to conclusions about causes, the relationships you observe in call center data may be useful for prediction:

- The details of a call that does not result in a pledge may be predictive of likelihood to pledge in a future year. For example, alumni who have cumulatively racked up minutes on the phone with your student callers that exceed the average may be better long-term prospects for your phone program in coming years. If this is true for your data, a model that incorporates this insight would be very useful for prioritizing and focusing your efforts, particularly if your non-donor prospect pool is large and your calling season is short.

- If call length is strongly associated with both pledging and upgrading, it will be useful in identifying prospects for annual giving at the leadership level.

- Ultimately, you'll also want to explore whether there's a relationship between call length and propensity to make a major gift or planned gift.

We cannot offer proof that these relationships exist in your data—you'll need to explore on your own. However, we've seen enough corroborative evidence in the data from other schools to suggest that ignoring call center data is a big mistake. We should add that the analysis above barely scratches the surface.

HOW MANY TIMES TO KEEP CALLING?

Phone solicitation is different from mail solicitation. It's high volume, meaning almost anyone can be called, particularly if calling is automated. It usually also costs less to call a prospect than mail a letter and a color-printed brochure. But reaching someone on the phone rarely happens with just one call. It takes multiple attempts to reach even loyal donors, and phonathon managers report that all prospects are getting harder and harder to reach by phone. As contact rates continue to fall year after year, some annual fund offices are considering eliminating their phone programs—a big mistake.

Often the question that phonathon managers face is not whom to call, but when to give up. How many attempts should your callers make before they "make contact" with an alum and either get a pledge or some other voice-to-voice response—or they give up and stop calling?

Most often these decisions are made on a segment-by-segment basis, and segments are put together using a set of selection criteria that include a combination of gift history (gave last year, didn't give last year but have some giving, or have no giving), degree type (what school or college the prospect graduated from), and other key attributes such as age group. These key attributes determine the message the prospect hears. That is, if they actually answer the phone.

Once the calling season is under way, contact rates begin to decline. Before long, most people who are prone to readily answering the phone have already done so. Time and resources may be running out, but the goal has not yet been reached. It's at this critical time that the phonathon manager decides it's time to start dropping segments out of the calling project, usually when he or she sees that the number of gifts and pledges from that segment have declined to a point where the segment looks like it's been exhausted. Some managers instead have a set number of call attempts to use on a segment before they will stop calling it—say, seven attempts for donors, three attempts per non-donor, and so on.

But is this optimal? Recall that one of the primary purposes of segmenting is to target each distinct group of alumni with an appropriate message. Messaging is not the same thing as receptivity to phone solicitation. Whenever a manager decides to give up on a segment, two errors are committed. First, the segment contains a lot of people who are highly resistant to answering the phone, and they should have been given up on a long time ago or never called at all; second, the segment contains a lot of people who are likely to answer the phone and likely to give, only it might take more effort to reach them and we shouldn't give up.

There would seem to be no winning in this situation. Unless, of course, we could somehow rank all prospects according to how likely they are to answer the phone, and then work that insight into our segmentation scheme.

We were able to gather some calling data from several institutions that may offer the beginnings of a methodology for just such an approach. With colleague John Sammis, the steps we took in our study included:

1. Using one school's data, we decided whether contact was made (or not) with 41,801 alumni who were recently called.

2. We calculated the percentage of contacts made and the pledge money raised for each of eight categories of call attempts: 1, 2, 3, 4, 5, 6, 7, and 8 or more.

3. We built an experimental predictive model for the likelihood of making contact with a given alum.

4. We used that model to see when it might (and might not) make sense to keep calling an individual alum.

Table 7.5 shows the results of the last call made. The first question we asked was, Which results can be classified as a "contact," and which cannot? The data came from a school using auto-dialing software that records the last result of every call (as coded by the caller), along with other data such as pledge details and the length of the conversation.

(By the way, manual calling programs can also benefit from data mining. There may be less call-result data to feed back into the modeling process than there would be in an automated system, but there is no reason why modeling cannot be used to segment intelligently in a manual program. If you have a manual program and you're calling tens of thousands of alumni—consider automating. Seriously.)

We agreed that these categories represented a successful contact, whether or not there was a gift or pledge as the result:

- Already Pledged
- No Pledge
- No Solicit
- Remove List
- Spec Pledge (i.e., Specified Pledge)
- Unsp Pledge (i.e., Unspecified Pledge, or "maybe")
- Do Not Call

TABLE 7.5 Frequency and Percentage Distributions for Results of Last Call Made to 41,801 Alums

RESULT	COUNT	%
No Pledge	12,424	29.72
AnsMachin	10,880	26.03
Disconnect	3,275	7.84
Wrong Num	3,152	7.54
Spec Pldg	2,491	5.96
No Answer	1,880	4.50
UnspPldg	1,734	4.15
Reassigned	1,475	3.53
Callback2	1,299	3.11
Out Cntry	626	1.50
Not Avail	610	1.46
DoNot Call	472	1.13
Already Pl	442	1.06
Busy	302	0.72
Hung Up	204	0.49
FAX2	133	0.32
Day	89	0.21
No Solicit	80	0.19
Prvcy Mgr	53	0.13
FAX	50	0.12
Callback	44	0.11
Remove Lst	42	0.10
NAO	39	0.09
Deceased	5	0.01

With each of these categories, there was a final "voice to voice" discussion between the caller and the alum. Sometimes this discussion had a pretty negative conclusion. If the alum says "do not call" or "remove from list" (1.13% and 0.10%, respectively), that's not great. "No pledge" (29.72%) and "unspecified pledge" (4.15%) are not so hot either, but at least they leave the door open for the future. "Already pledged" (1.06%)? What can you say to that one? "And which decade was that, sir?"

Now let's look at how many call attempts had been placed to each alum. We said that we grouped all alumni in the sample according to how many calls they'd received before they were either contacted or the phonathon manager gave up on them or ran out of time to call. Table 7.6 and Figure 7.13 show the number and percentage of contacts made for each group of "number of attempts." After that, the next table and chart show the pledge rate for the same groups (Table 7.7 and Figure 7.14).

We've taken a hard look at both these tables and figures, and we've concluded that they don't really offer helpful guidelines for deciding when to stop calling at this school. Why? We don't see a definitive number of attempts where it would make sense to stop. To get specific, let's go over the attempts:

- 1st attempt: This attempt clearly yielded the most alums contacted (6,023) and the most dollars pledged ($79,316). However, stopping here

TABLE 7.6 Number of Contacts Made and Percentage Contact Made for Each of Eight Categories of Attempts

# OF ATTEMPTS	COUNT	CONTACTS MADE	% CONTACTS MADE
1	12,201	6,023	49.4%
2	6,400	3,870	60.5%
3	4,318	2,705	62.6%
4	4,347	1,859	42.8%
5	3,210	1,269	39.5%
6	6,591	895	13.6%
7	2,203	380	17.2%
8 or More	2,531	684	27.0%

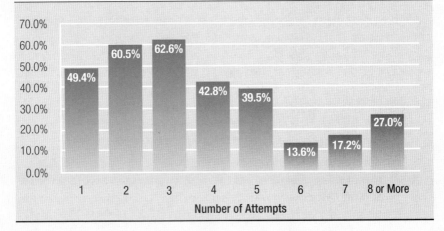

FIGURE 7.13 Percentage Contact Made for Each of Eight Categories of Attempts

TABLE 7.7 Total Pledge Dollars and Mean Pledge Dollars Received for Each of Eight Categories of Attempts

# OF ATTEMPTS	COUNT	TOTAL PLEDGE $ RECEIVED	MEAN PLEDGE $ RECEIVED
1	12,201	$79,316	$6.50
2	6,400	$49,385	$7.72
3	4,318	$31,814	$7.37
4	4,347	$19,885	$4.57
5	3,210	$14,120	$4.40
6	6,591	$9,050	$1.37
7	2,203	$7,880	$3.58
8 or More	2,531	$19,075	$7.54

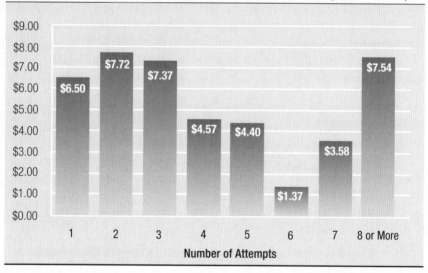

FIGURE 7.14 Mean Pledge Dollars Received for Each of Eight Categories of Attempts

would make little sense, if only for the fact that the attempt yielded only a third of the $230,526 that would eventually be raised.

- 2nd attempt: Should we stop here? Well, $49,385 was raised, and the contact rate has now jumped from about 50% to over 60%. We'd say keep going.

- 3rd attempt: How about here? More than $30,000 raised and the contact rate has jumped even a bit higher. We're not stopping.

- 4th attempt: Here things start to go downhill a bit. The contact rate has fallen to about 43%, and the total pledges raised have fallen below $20,000. However, if we stop here, we'll be leaving more money on the table.

- 5th attempt through 8 or more attempts: What can we say? Clearly the contact rates are not great for these attempts; they never get above the 40% level. Still, money for pledges continues to come in—more than $50,000.

Even before we looked at the attempts data, we were convinced that the right question was not "How many call attempts should be made before callers stop?" The right question was "How many call attempts should be made with which alumni?" In other words, with some alums it makes sense to keep calling until you reach them and have a chance to ask for a pledge. With others, that's not a good strategy. In fact, it's a waste of time and energy and money.

So, how do you identify those alumni who should be called a lot and those who shouldn't? We firmly believed it would be possible to build a predictive model for making contact with alumni, one that could give some idea of who is highly likely to be successfully contacted and who isn't. The trick would be finding the right predictors—the right attributes that are most strongly associated with the behavior of answering the phone.

For each of the 41,801 alumni included in this study we amassed data on the following variables:

- Email (whether or not the alum had an email address listed in the database)
- Lifetime hard credit dollars given to the school
- Preferred class year
- Year of last gift made over the phone (if one was ever made)
- Marital status missing (whether or not there was no marital code whatsoever for the alum in the marital status field)
- Event attendance (whether or not the alum had ever attended an event since graduation)

With these variables we used a regression analysis to combine the variables into a score that could be used to predict an alum's likelihood of being contacted by a caller. The outcome variable was a binary variable: "contact made." Each prospect could have only one of two states (contacted/not contacted), because, although multiple call attempts might be made to an alum, each alum can be contacted only once. The result of a contact might be a pledge, no pledge, maybe, or "do not call"—but in any case, the result is binary.

Because regression is hard to get one's arms around, we won't try to explain that part of what we did. We'll just ask you to trust us that it worked pretty well. What we will do is show you the relationship between three of the above variables and whether or not contact was made with an alum. This will give you a sense of why we included them as predictors in the model.

We'll start with lifetime giving. Table 7.8 and Figure 7.15 show that as lifetime giving goes up, the likelihood of making contact with an alum also goes up. Notice that callers are more than twice as likely to make contact with alums who have given $120 or more lifetime (75.4%) than they are to make contact with alums whose lifetime giving is zero (34.9%). By *lifetime giving,* we mean giving via any solicitation method, not just by phone.

TABLE 7.8   Number of Contacts Made and Percentage Contact Made for Three Levels of Lifetime Giving

LEVELS OF LIFETIME GIVING	COUNT	CONTACTS MADE	% CONTACT MADE
$0	33,271	11,623	34.9%
$1–$119	4,308	2,878	66.8%
$120 or More	4,222	3,184	75.4%

FIGURE 7.15   Percentage Contact Made for Each of Three Levels of Lifetime Giving

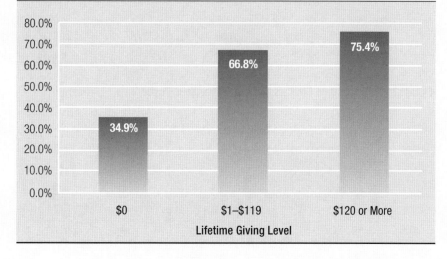

How about Preferred Class Year? The relationship between this variable and contact rate is a bit complicated. You'll see in Table 7.9 that with the aid of stats software we've divided class year into 10 roughly equal size groups called "deciles." The first decile includes alums whose preferred class year goes from 1964 to 1978. The second decile includes alums whose preferred class year goes from 1979 to 1985. The tenth decile includes alums whose preferred class year goes from 2008 to 2010.

A look at Figure 7.16 shows that contact rate is highest with the older alums and then gradually falls off as the class years get more recent. However, the rate rises a bit with the most recent alums. Without going into detail, we can tell you that we're able to use this less-than-straight-line relationship in building our model.

TABLE 7.9 Percentage Contact Made by Class Year Decile

CLASS YEAR DECILE	COUNT	FIRST YEAR	LAST YEAR	% CONTACT MADE
1	3,527	1964	1978	63.5%
2	3,718	1979	1985	57.7%
3	3,879	1986	1990	54.2%
4	4,068	1991	1994	46.2%
5	3,538	1995	1997	38.0%
6	4,037	1998	2000	34.2%
7	3,003	2001	2002	33.8%
8	5,971	2003	2005	31.0%
9	4,185	2006	2007	32.7%
10	5,875	2008	2010	40.2%

FIGURE 7.16 Percentage Contact Made by Class Year Decile

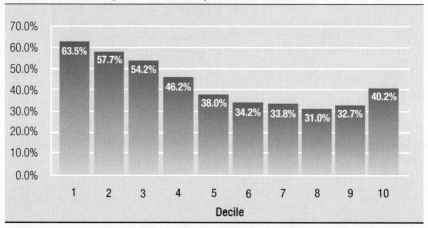

The third variable we'll look at is Event Attendance. Table 7.10 and Figure 7.17 show that, although relatively few alums (2,211) attended an event versus those who did not (35,590), the contact rate was considerably higher for the event attenders than the non-attenders: 58.3% versus 41.4%.

The predictive model we built generated a very granular score for each of the 41,801 alums in the study. To make it easier to see how these scores looked and worked, we collapsed the alumni into 10 roughly equal size groups (deciles, again) based on the scores. The higher the decile, the better the scores. (These deciles are, of course, different from the deciles we talked about for Preferred Class Year.)

TABLE 7.10 Percentage Contact Made by Event Attendance

EVENT ATTENDANCE	COUNT	% CONTACT MADE
No	39,590	41.4%
Yes	2,211	58.3%

FIGURE 7.17 Percentage Contact Made by Event Attendance

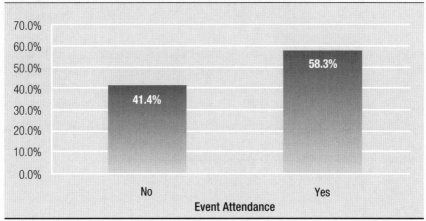

Shortly we'll talk about how we used these decile scores as a possible method for deciding when to stop calling. But first, let's look at how these scores are related to both contact rate and pledging. Table 7.11 and Figure 7.18 deal with contact rate.

Clearly, there is a strong relationship between the scores and whether contact was made. Maybe the most striking aspect of these displays is the contrast between contact rate for alums in the 10th decile and that for those in the first decile: 79.9% versus 19.2%. In practical terms, this means that, over time in this school, your callers are going to make contact with only one in every five alums in the first decile. But in the 10th decile? They should make contact with four in every five alums.

TABLE 7.11   Number of Contacts Made and Percentage Contact Made by Contact Score Decile

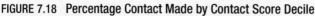

CONTACT SCORE DECILE	COUNT	CONTACTS MADE	% CONTACT MADE
1	3,833	735	19.2%
2	3,625	1,018	28.1%
3	5,041	1,463	29.0%
4	3,331	1,077	32.3%
5	4,899	1,658	33.8%
6	4,233	1,627	38.4%
7	4,206	1,838	43.7%
8	4,273	2,183	51.1%
9	4,180	2,748	65.7%
10	4,180	3,338	79.9%

FIGURE 7.18   Percentage Contact Made by Contact Score Decile

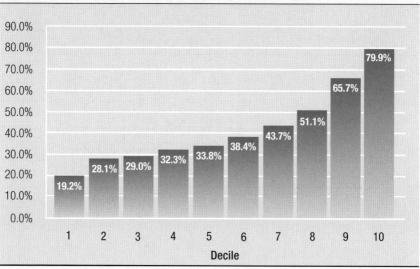

How about pledge rates? We didn't build this model to predict pledge rates. However, look at Table 7.12 and Figure 7.19. Notice the striking differences between the lower and upper deciles in terms of total dollars pledged. For example, we can compare the total pledge dollars received for the bottom 20% of alums called (deciles 1 and 2) and the top 20% of alums called (deciles 9 and 10): about $2,700 versus almost $200,000.

TABLE 7.12 Total Pledge Dollars and Mean Pledge Dollars Received by Contact Score Decile

CONTACT SCORE DECILE	COUNT	TOTAL PLEDGE $ RECEIVED	MEAN PLEDGE $ RECEIVED
1	3,833	$1,990	$0.52
2	3,625	$750	$0.21
3	5,041	$2,225	$0.44
4	3,331	$3,490	$1.05
5	4,899	$3,855	$0.79
6	4,233	$5,710	$1.35
7	4,206	$5,510	$1.31
8	4,273	$8,645	$2.02
9	4,180	$49,897	$11.94
10	4,180	$148,453	$35.52

FIGURE 7.19 Mean Pledge Dollars Received by Contact Score Decile

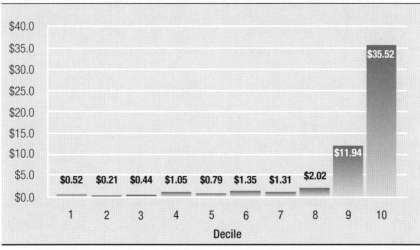

Our big question, the one we set out to answer, is When does it make sense to stop calling a prospect? We have a lot of tables and figures for you to look at. Specifically, you'll see:

- Both the number of contacts made and the contact rate by decile score level for each of the first six attempts. (We decided to cut things off at the sixth attempt for reasons we think you'll find obvious.)

- A table that shows the total pledge dollars raised for each attempt by decile score level.

Don't be put off by all the detail in these tables and charts. Go ahead and browse through them, and then we will tell you what we see. We believe that a few obvious facts emerge.

The First Attempt

TABLE 7.13   Number of Contacts Made and Percentage Contact Made
by Contact Score Decile for the First Attempt

CONTACT SCORE DECILE	COUNT	CONTACTS MADE	% CONTACT MADE
1	1,182	224	19.0%
2	985	332	33.7%
3	1,290	493	38.2%
4	980	392	40.0%
5	1,477	574	38.9%
6	1,372	602	43.9%
7	1,253	616	49.2%
8	1,277	729	57.1%
9	1,133	926	81.7%
10	1,252	1,135	90.7%

FIGURE 7.20   Percentage Contact Made by Contact Score Decile
for the First Attempt

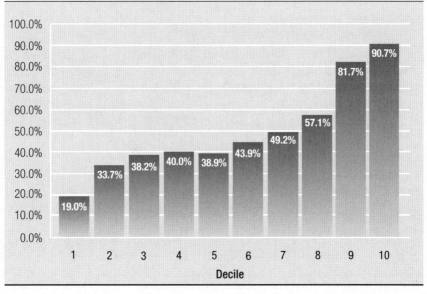

The Second Attempt

TABLE 7.14   Number of Contacts Made and Percentage Contact Made
by Contact Score Decile for the Second Attempt

CONTACT SCORE DECILE	COUNT	CONTACTS MADE	% CONTACT MADE
1	665	158	23.8%
2	699	221	31.6%
3	700	362	51.7%
4	448	230	51.3%
5	671	347	51.7%
6	582	348	59.8%
7	579	421	72.7%
8	645	500	77.5%
9	658	567	86.2%
10	753	716	95.1%

FIGURE 7.21   Percentage Contact Made by Contact Score Decile
for the Second Attempt

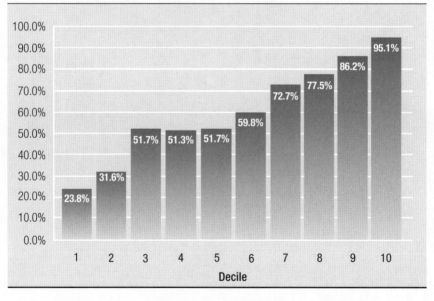

The Third Attempt

TABLE 7.15   Number of Contacts Made and Percentage Contact Made
by Contact Score Decile for the Third Attempt

CONTACT SCORE DECILE	COUNT	CONTACTS MADE	% CONTACT MADE
1	317	121	38.2%
2	282	175	62.1%
3	541	235	43.4%
4	341	158	46.3%
5	548	289	52.7%
6	501	270	53.9%
7	422	299	70.9%
8	437	329	75.3%
9	460	394	85.7%
10	469	435	92.8%

FIGURE 7.22   Percentage Contact Made by Contact Score Decile
for the Third Attempt

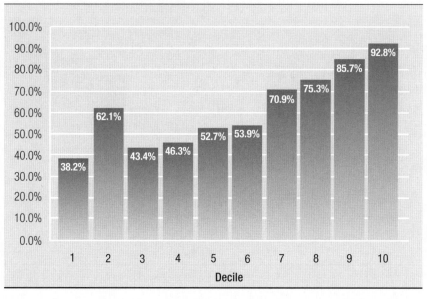

The Fourth Attempt

TABLE 7.16   Number of Contacts Made and Percentage Contact Made
by Contact Score Decile for the Fourth Attempt

CONTACT SCORE DECILE	COUNT	CONTACTS MADE	% CONTACT MADE
1	420	91	21.7%
2	304	118	38.8%
3	736	169	23.0%
4	408	122	29.9%
5	571	195	34.2%
6	459	191	41.6%
7	412	213	51.7%
8	321	212	66.0%
9	348	259	74.4%
10	368	289	78.5%

FIGURE 7.23   Percentage Contact Made by Contact Score Decile
for the Fourth Attempt

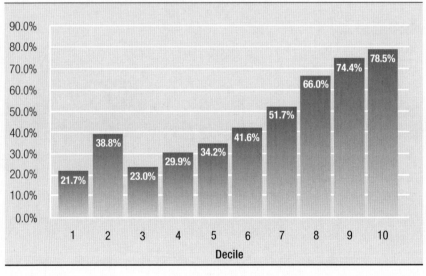

The Fifth Attempt

TABLE 7.17 Number of Contacts Made and Percentage Contact Made
by Contact Score Decile for the Fifth Attempt

CONTACT SCORE DECILE	COUNT	CONTACTS MADE	% CONTACT MADE
1	348	71	20.4%
2	259	94	36.3%
3	465	128	27.5%
4	345	89	25.8%
5	415	117	28.2%
6	337	104	30.9%
7	304	126	41.4%
8	240	150	62.5%
9	273	198	72.5%
10	224	192	85.7%

FIGURE 7.24 Percentage Contact Made by Contact Score Decile
for the Fifth Attempt

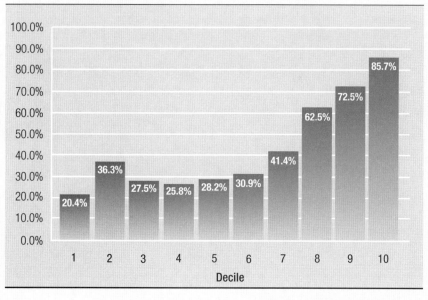

The Sixth Attempt

TABLE 7.18 Number of Contacts Made and Percentage Contact Made
by Contact Score Decile for the Sixth Attempt

CONTACT SCORE DECILE	COUNT	CONTACTS MADE	% CONTACT MADE
1	690	56	8.1%
2	899	63	7.0%
3	1,114	70	6.3%
4	569	68	12.0%
5	697	83	11.9%
6	630	69	11.0%
7	820	89	10.9%
8	676	118	17.5%
9	314	128	40.8%
10	182	151	83.0%

FIGURE 7.25 Percentage Contact Made by Contact Score Decile
for the Sixth Attempt

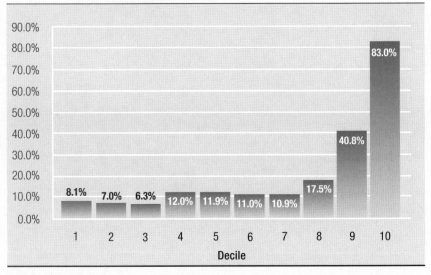

This is what we see:
- For each of the six attempts, the contact rate increases as the score
  decile increases. There are some bumps and inconsistencies along the
  way (see Figure 7.22, for example), but this is clearly the overall pattern
  for each of the attempts.

- For all the attempts, the contact rate for the lowest 20% of scores (deciles 1 and 2) is always substantially lower than the contact rate for the highest 20% of scores (deciles 9 and 10).

- Once we reach the sixth attempt, the contact rates fall off dramatically for all but the 10th decile.

Now take a look at Table 7.19, which shows the total pledge money raised for each attempt (including the seventh attempt and eight or more attempts) by score decile. You can also look at Table 7.20, which shows the same information but with the amounts exceeding $1,000 outlined in black.

We could talk about these two tables in some detail, but we'd rather just say, "Wow!"

TABLE 7.19 Total Pledge Dollars Raised In Each Attempt by Contact Score Decile

DECILE	1ST ATTEMPT	2ND ATTEMPT	3RD ATTEMPT	4TH ATTEMPT	5TH ATTEMPT	6TH ATTEMPT	7TH ATTEMPT	8 OR MORE ATTEMPTS
1	$685	$225	$590	$60	$0	$430	$0	$0
2	$235	$185	$135	$50	$100	$45	$0	$0
3	$775	$735	$290	$200	$205	$20	$0	$0
4	$1,680	$725	$420	$210	$145	$290	$20	$0
5	$1,410	$1,025	$500	$450	$370	$70	$0	$30
6	$2,255	$1,145	$630	$990	$380	$140	$170	$0
7	$2,015	$1,025	$990	$240	$740	$100	$350	$50
8	$3,510	$2,165	$805	$655	$615	$430	$10	$455
9	$14,895	$10,420	$7,254	$3,095	$3,043	$2,025	$2,095	$7,070
10	$51,856	$31,735	$20,200	$13,935	$8,522	$5,500	$5,235	$11,470

TABLE 7.20 Total Pledge Dollars Raised In Each Attempt by Contact Score Decile with Pledge Amounts Greater Than $1,000 Outlined in Black

DECILE	1ST ATTEMPT	2ND ATTEMPT	3RD ATTEMPT	4TH ATTEMPT	5TH ATTEMPT	6TH ATTEMPT	7TH ATTEMPT	8 OR MORE ATTEMPTS
1	$685	$225	$590	$60	$0	$430	$0	$0
2	$235	$185	$135	$50	$100	$45	$0	$0
3	$775	$735	$290	$200	$205	$20	$0	$0
4	$1,680	$725	$420	$210	$145	$290	$20	$0
5	$1,410	$1,025	$500	$450	$370	$70	$0	$30
6	$2,255	$1,145	$630	$990	$380	$140	$170	$0
7	$2,015	$1,025	$990	$240	$740	$100	$350	$50
8	$3,510	$2,165	$805	$655	$615	$430	$10	$455
9	$14,895	$10,420	$7,254	$3,095	$3,043	$2,025	$2,095	$7,070
10	$51,856	$31,735	$20,200	$13,935	$8,522	$5,500	$5,235	$11,470

So then, how many attempts should your callers make before they "make contact" with an alum and either get a pledge or some other voice to voice response—or they give up and stop calling? Our analysis points to a few suggestions:

One: There is no across-the-board number of attempts that you should apply in your program, or even to any segment in your program; the number of attempts you make to reach an alum very much depends on who that alum is.

Two: There are some alumni who should be attempted repeatedly, because you will eventually reach them and (probably) receive a pledge from them. Even someone who picks up the phone this year and says "no" is still a better prospect in the long run than someone who never answers the call. On the other hand, there are other alumni who should be called only once, or not at all.

And three: If the school we used for this analysis is at all representative of other institutions that do calling, all across North America huge amounts of time and money are wasted trying to reach alumni with whom contact will never be made nor will any pledges be raised.

You might notice that we haven't mentioned a key component of decision-making with regard to solicitation: the cost of solicitation, and the associated return on investment. A few people who have seen our analysis have asked us, Wouldn't it make sense to cut off calling a segment once "profitability" reached some unacceptably low point?

Cost is important; but unfortunately, cost accounting can be complicated even within the bounds of a single program, let alone compared across institutions. Money for student wages may come from one source, money for technology and software support from another, and regular expenses such as phone and network charges from another. If you realize efficiencies in spending and reallocate dollars to other areas, does it makes sense to include them in your cost accounting? We're not sure.

Here's another way to look at it. Your budget determines how many weeks of calling are possible. Therefore, the limiting factor is actually *time.* Many (or most) phone programs do little more than call as many people as possible in the time available. They call with no regard for prospects' probability of giving (aside from favoring recent donors), spreading their limited resources evenly over all prospects—that is, not optimally.

If you spend more time calling prospects who are likely to answer the phone and less time calling prospects who aren't, then you're already taking a big step toward maximizing on your investment. ROI is important; but if you're not segmenting properly, you're always going to end up simultaneously giving up on high-value prospects prematurely *and* hanging on to low-value prospects beyond the limit of profitability.

As with many other applications of predictive modeling, it's all about focusing limited resources where they will do the most good.

Dealing with Annual Fund Prospect Attrition

Speaking of calling certain prospects less often, there's a group of people whom we just don't call at all: the ones who have asked us not to contact them. We assume that alumni who tell their alma maters not to ask them for money intended two things: (1) Don't ask me, and (2) I'm not going to give you anything. Is that really the case?

Every year, a large number of alumni will tell us they're not interested in hearing from us again. Some of them want to cut all ties, others just don't want to be asked for money. Maybe we called them just as they were sitting down to eat, and they see us as just another annoying telemarketer. Maybe we sent them one email too many, and they asked to be removed from our mailing list. Or maybe they just don't want our mail anymore. Annual giving and alumni records offices will have various codes to cover these preferences. Our next study looks at the code (or group of codes) called "Do Not Solicit."

These codes are a hot topic. Restrictions on solicitation and contact are coming under increased scrutiny as annual giving programs become more aware of attrition in prospect pools. In many cases, these codes were applied years ago and not always for good reasons. We may be tempted to consider reestablishing contact. Is this wise? Should we not respect people's wishes?

Well, not all contact restrictions are requested by prospects. Some have been assigned by the institution. It is common for prospects assigned to major gift officers to be coded "no contact by annual fund." Unfortunately, these codes may persist in the database long after they are relevant; from then on, the prospect may go unsolicited. Even requests from alumni might be considered provisional. In a fit of pique at being called at an inconvenient time, alumni will request not to be solicited and then completely forget that they have done so. (Quite a few people who hang up on student callers and end up coded Do Not Call are actually good by-mail donors. They just haven't communicated their preference.) Or they will ask not to be contacted in any way and then later complain they aren't getting their alumni magazine or invitations to events. Sound familiar?

Contact restrictions can be a sensitive subject, so proceed with caution, certainly. But the analysis to follow shows that it is possible for you to identify a segment of DNS-coded people for whom you can attempt to re-initiate contact, with reasonable assurance of success and minimal backlash.

RETHINKING "DO NOT SOLICIT"

Not long ago, a good friend and colleague of Peter's sent him some data for a project. Of the 50,000 or so records she sent, more than 7,000 had a "do not solicit" tag. Okay, that's seems clear: Don't call 'em, don't send 'em letters or emails, and definitely don't go knocking on their doors just because you happen to be in the neighborhood.

But Peter is nosy. He checked to see if any of those 7,000 or so had ever given the school any money. It turns out that a little over a third of them *had* given some money. He couldn't tell how much because his friend had not given him dollar amounts, only whether or not they'd ever given a hard credit gift to the school. The actual amounts were not relevant to the project.

Peter couldn't stop there. He started digging around to see what some of the differences were between the ones who'd given and the ones who hadn't. The differences he found were quite interesting. If you follow Peter's example and check your own school's data, you just might make similar discoveries.

In a moment we will take a look at Figures 7.26–31, showing some variables on which DNS alumni differ markedly when it comes to giving. It's important to point out that we don't know *when* or under *what circumstances* any of these alums told the school they did not want to be solicited. For example,

- Did they do it recently or a long time ago?

- Did they do it on a permanent basis or just temporarily? It's possible that some of them are parents of kids attending the school and their attitude for the next four years is, "Hey, I'm paying an arm and a leg for tuition. Until I'm done with that, please don't go asking me for money while I'm in hock up to my underwear."

- Are they bent out of shape over the beloved football coach who was finally let go after 10 consecutive losing seasons—something they may eventually get beyond? Or is it simply a case of "I'll give you something, maybe a lot, when I'm ready. In the meantime, don't bug me"?

Again, we don't know. But before any advancement person uses the results of a predictive model like this one, he should consider these sorts of possibilities. More about that later.

Let's take a walk through the figures.

We see in Figure 7.26 that there are huge differences in the giving rates among three types of alumni. Undergraduate alums are almost twice as likely to give as graduate alums and more than six times as likely to give as non-degreed alums.

Figure 7.27 shows us that alums who have attended at least one reunion are two and a half times as likely to give as alums who have never attended a reunion.

FIGURE 7.26   Percentage of "Do Not Solicit" Alums Who Have Ever Made a Gift by Alumni Type

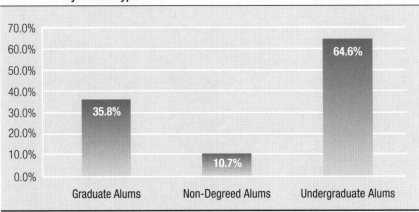

FIGURE 7.27   Percentage of "Do Not Solicit" Alums Who Have Ever Made A Gift by Reunion Attendance

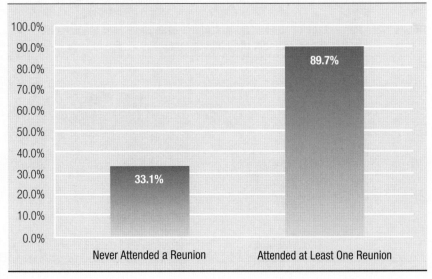

Looking at Figure 7.28, we see that alums who have never attended an event are less than half as likely to give as alums who've attended one event and about a third as likely to give as alums who have attended two or more events.

In Figure 7.29 we see that alums who are members of the online community are twice as likely to give as alums who are not members.

FIGURE 7.28 Percentage of "Do Not Solicit" Alums Who Have Ever Made a Gift by Event Attendance

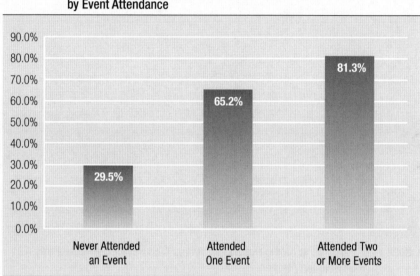

FIGURE 7.29 Percentage of "Do Not Solicit" Alums Who Have Ever Made A Gift by Whether a Member of Online Community

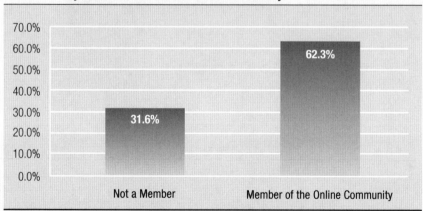

Alums who were members of a Greek organization as undergrads are almost twice as likely to give as alums who were not Greek members, as we see in Figure 7.30.

Alums who are children of alums are two and a half times as likely to give as alums whose parents are not alums. Check out Figure 7.31.

Clearly, these figures (and several Peter hasn't included) show there are a number of variables in the alumni database at this school that can be used to predict which "do not solicit" alums *may* be more likely to give in the future. One way to find out if we're right is to (a) build a model that yields a "likelihood of giving" score for each of these alums and (b) begin testing the model.

FIGURE 7.30   Percentage of "Do Not Solicit" Alums Who Ever Made a Gift by Whether a Member of a Greek Organization as an Undergrad

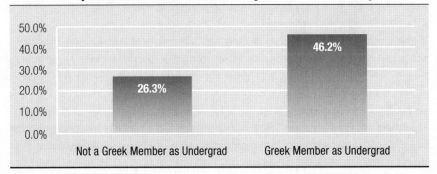

FIGURE 7.31   Percentage of "Do Not Solicit" Alums Who Have Ever Made a Gift by Whether a Child of an Alum

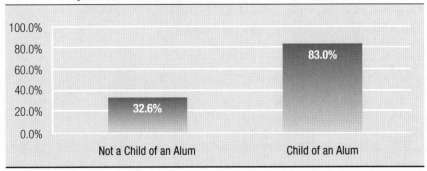

Knowing some of the attributes that distinguish donors from non-donors, as suggested by the figures above, you can build a predictive model that creates a score for every alum in your database who is coded Do Not Solicit. The equation could go like this, adding 1 to the score for each positive predictor, and subtracting 1 for each negative predictor:

DONOR LIKELIHOOD SCORE = Undergrad alum – non-degree alum
+ reunion attendance + attended 2 or more events – never attended an event
+ online community member + Greek membership+ child of an alum + 2

This equation will make sense if you review the charts above. We *add* to the score if the alum has an undergraduate degree, has attended at least one reunion, has attended at least two events, is a member of the online community, was a Greek member, or is the son or daughter of an alum. We *subtract* from the score if the alum never earned a degree or never attended an event.

Why do we add 2 on the end? Because the lowest possible score is –2, so adding two makes the minimum score zero, which is a little neater. And the maximum score that an alum could earn would therefore be 8. Alumni with very high scores (say, 6 to 8) have a probability of giving that is significantly higher than that of alumni with lower scores.

Readers with some knowledge of statistics might consider a different option for creating a predictive model: using multiple regression, which is what Peter did for this study. The subject of multiple regression could fill many books (and does), so we will not explain it here. Very briefly, regression uses the same data as inputs, but adjusts the resulting score for differences in the strength of individual predictors, as well as adjusting for overlapping effects among those predictors.

Using multiple regression, Peter created a score for each alum where EVER GAVE (0/1) was the outcome variable and where the variables you see above as well as the following were the predictor variables:

- Count of current volunteer activities

- Count of past volunteer activities

- Year the alum graduated (or should have if he or she had completed a degree "on time")

The model generated well over 2,500 different score levels into which the 7,393 alums could fall—way too many for anybody to get their conceptual arms around. The adjusted R squared for the model was about 36%. (Again, don't worry if you don't know what R squared means.)

Peter divided the 2,695 score levels into 10 equal-sized groups (deciles), each containing about 740 alumni. As you look at Table 7.21, you'll see these groups varied some in size. In decile 1 (the lowest scoring 10% of alums), there are 726 people. In decile 10 (the highest scoring 10% of alums), there are 739 people.

TABLE 7.21   Frequency Breakdown of "Do Not Solicit" Alums by Score Decile

SCORE DECILE	COUNT	SCORE DECILE	COUNT
1	726	6	742
2	730	7	739
3	758	8	740
4	743	9	740
5	736	10	739

If the model is to be useful in identifying DNS alums who are likely to give, the number and percentage of givers should increase as the deciles increase. A look at Table 7.22 and Figure 7.32 show that these numbers and percentages do just that. For example, in the first decile, of the 726 alums, only 12 (1.7%) have ever given anything to the school. In the 10th decile, of the 739 alums, 649 (87.8%) have given to the school.

Higher education advancement offices ignore most of the data they have on their alumni as they go about the business of raising money from them, so it is more than likely that this sort of study has never been done at your institution. Who would have thought there would be such striking differences between givers and non-givers who ask not to be asked? Not Peter. He just stumbled onto it because he was playing around with data that had been put together for a totally different reason. Alumni databases are *oceans* of data that could help us save a lot of money and generate a lot more revenue for worthy missions. But with the *drops* of analysis we're currently doing on all that data, we're not saving all that much money nor generating that much more revenue.

Try to build a predictive giving model for your own "Do not solicit" alums. If you're not proficient with using statistical software, find somebody in your school who is and get that person to help you. If you have an Office of Institutional Research (or some similarly titled entity), that's a good place to look. Just make sure the person you choose grasps the basic idea of what you're trying to do and has the capacity to explain technical stuff in plain English.

Then do some in-depth research on the high-scoring alums who emerge from your model, especially those who've been generous givers over the years. Share the names with some of your colleagues, whether they're involved in the annual fund, prospect research, or part of your cadre of gifts officers. There might be at least one alum who will pop out of the mix who is ready for an appeal, with the right strategy.

Perhaps the first touch should not be an ask. Try an event invitation or some other communication from the alumni office. Study the results.

If your database allows it, start tracking the *source* of DNS and other exclusion codes in the database. A key aspect of coding the source is differentiating between alumni-requested exclusions ("I don't want any more phone calls") and exclusions assigned by the institution ("Don't talk to my major-gift prospect"). Clearly

TABLE 7.22   Number and Percentage of "Do Not Solicit" Alums Who Gave
by Score Decile

SCORE DECILE	COUNT	# OF GIVERS	% OF GIVERS
1	726	12	1.7%
2	730	27	3.7%
3	758	48	6.3%
4	743	115	15.5%
5	736	146	19.8%
6	742	222	29.9%
7	739	340	46.0%
8	740	414	55.9%
9	740	523	70.7%
10	739	649	87.8%

FIGURE 7.32   Percentage of "Do Not Solicit" Alums Who Gave by Score Decile

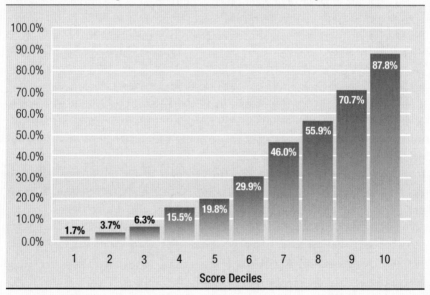

we need to honor the wishes of alumni, but the validity of our own determinations should be questioned regularly. Was that angrily hung-up phone five years ago still a good enough reason to avoid calling? Were a lot of codes being created across swaths of alumni at the request of development officers? (And how many of those "assigned" alumni have actually been contacted or visited?)

In short, make sure your codes are specific, explicit, sourced, and certain. If they're solid, honor them to the hilt. If not, consider them time-limited and subject to review.

chapter 8

Major Giving
Enriching the Prospect Pool

L et's say you're a prospect researcher in higher education. You're getting some pressure—from your boss, from some of the gift officers you work with, maybe the campaign director—to come up with a list of new prospects. They use different words, but their message is clear:

"We've picked the low-hanging fruit. We don't want to keep going back to the same alumni who've been helping us out in a big way for a long time. We need to find some new people who have the capacity and willingness to make a nice gift. Maybe not a huge gift, but a nice gift."

You've been working in the field awhile, so this isn't the first time you've faced this problem, nor is it the first time somebody has offered advice on how to solve it. Truth be told, you may have gotten too much advice:

- "You haven't done a screening for five years. You need to do a new one."

- "Our company has gotten very sophisticated about predictive modeling as well as gift capacity ratings. Use us."

- "You're not using social media resources effectively. Facebook and LinkedIn are great places to find out about alums who have lots of financial resources and are philanthropically inclined."

- "You need to learn how to do data mining and predictive modeling or add somebody to your staff who already knows how to do it."

It's not that any of this advice is bad, even if it comes from a vendor whose goal is to get some of your business. The problem is that you, or the person you report to, has to sift through this advice and make some kind of decision, even if that decision is to do nothing different from what you're currently doing. In the example that follows, we hope to make prospect identification less complicated, not more.

case study five   **MAJOR GIFT PROSPECT IDENTIFICATION**

What we've done here is use some data, from a large public higher education institution, to walk you through a simple process for finding new prospects. Before we do that, let's start off with three assumptions:

- You have fairly recent gift capacity ratings for several thousand of your solicitable alumni, some of whom you think may be good, untapped prospects.

- You have access to someone who can develop a simple score for all those alums with respect to their affinity to give to your school.

- You have reasonably good profiles on each of these alums. That is, those profiles include information like lifetime hard credit dollars given, date and amount of last gift, date and amount of first gift, what gift officers have ever been assigned to those alums and when, the most recent occupation of the alum, and so on.

Here are the steps we want to take you through:

1. Look at the distribution of gift capacity ratings for the alumni you've recently screened.
2. Look at the giving data for these alumni by gift capacity ratings.
3. Build a simple affinity model using some very basic information stored on each alum.
4. Pick a small group of alums who have a high capacity rating, a high affinity rating, and are not currently assigned to a gift officer.
5. Look closely at the alums in this small group and identify some who may deserve more scrutiny.

We'll go through each of these steps in detail. First, let's look at the distribution of gift capacity ratings for the alums you've recently screened. Whenever you have a field of data (whether it comes from your own database or has been delivered to you by a vendor), it's a good idea to make a frequency distribution of that variable. There are a couple of reasons for doing this:

- You get a big-picture look at the variable. Our experience is that most people in higher education advancement don't do this for the many variables they have in their alumni databases. For example, let's say you asked the average associate vice president for advancement in a college or university this question: "What percentage of your solicitable alums have given $100 or less lifetime hard credit?" Our bet is that the vast majority would have no idea of what the correct answer was; moreover, they would be shocked if you told them.

- You get a chance to see if there is anything out of the ordinary about the data that's worth further exploration. Here's a good example. When doing predictive modeling, we look closely at the variable "preferred class year." It's a measure of how long alums have been out of school, and it's a reasonably good measure of age. It's not at all uncommon for us to encounter thousands of records coded as "0000" or, say, "1700." Call it a hunch, but we're pretty sure those folks didn't graduate the year Christ was born, nor 75 years or so before the Declaration of Independence got signed. When we encounter a problem like this, of course, we ask the advancement services people we're working with what those codes mean. The answers vary. Sometimes such codes indicate alums who are non-degreed. Sometimes they indicate alums who simply received a certain kind of certificate. Or they indicate something else. The important thing is that we ask; we clear up the mystery.

Table 8.1 shows a distribution of the gift capacity ratings for a group of about 22,000 alumni in the public higher education institution we mentioned earlier. Figure 8.1 displays the same distribution graphically. Take a minute or two to look at both of them. Then you can compare what you see with what we noticed.

For us, two things about this data stand out:

1. Some of the data is a little hard to believe. Let's take a look at Group 1 in Table 8.1. There are 1,123 records in this group. They comprise alums with the lowest 5% of gift capacity ratings. If you look at the "min" column, you'll see that the lowest gift capacity rating is one dollar. Really? That alum must be down on his or her luck. You can't see all the data in this distribution the way we can, but there are a total of 11 alums whose gift capacity is listed as being under $100. Obviously, you should be suspicious of such ratings. Contacting the vendor who generated them is a must. And politely staying after them until you get an acceptable answer is the right thing to do.

TABLE 8.1   Estimated $ Gift Capacity for More Than 22,000 Alumni Divided
into 20 Groups of Roughly 5% Each

GROUP	COUNT	TOTAL GIFT CAPACITY	MEDIAN CAPACITY	MIN	MAX
1	1,123	2,666,720	2,414	1	3,976
2	1,122	5,981,880	5,333	3,977	6,571
3	1,123	8,641,020	7,681	6,574	8,812
4	1,122	11,310,200	10,128	8,817	11,381
5	1,123	14,293,500	12,742	11,384	14,095
6	1,123	17,286,600	15,364	14,096	16,709
7	1,119	20,200,600	18,094	16,710	19,323
8	1,126	23,164,200	20,585	19,327	21,839
9	1,122	25,931,600	23,128	21,841	24,408
10	1,122	28,866,200	25,675	24,410	27,094
11	1,124	31,959,200	28,433	27,097	29,808
12	1,122	35,088,500	31,281	29,809	32,765
13	1,122	38,462,800	34,252	32,768	35,882
14	1,123	42,277,600	37,678	35,886	39,415
15	1,122	46,221,700	41,146	39,417	43,265
16	1,124	51,381,900	45,556	43,273	48,483
17	1,122	58,083,600	51,702	48,485	55,674
18	1,123	68,510,600	60,561	55,682	67,920
19	1,122	100,034,000	87,686	67,930	116,538
20	1,123	405,958,000	192,384	116,629	45,308,100

FIGURE 8.1   Estimated Median $ Gift Capacity for More Than 22,000 Alumni Divided
into 20 Groups of Roughly 5% Each

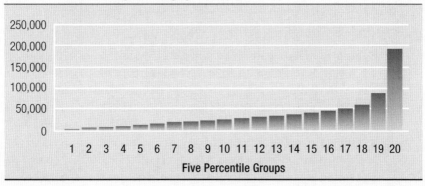

2. The capacity ratings rise slowly until we get to the top 10% of alums. There's nothing particularly surprising about this. However, it is interesting (without showing you all the arithmetic) that, of the roughly one billion dollars of total gift capacity for these alums, more than half a billion of that gift capacity resides with the top 10% of the alums.

Now we will look at the giving data for these alumni, by wealth capacity ratings. We want to see how those capacity ratings are related to the money the same alumni have given to the school.

We'll start with Table 8.2. The two columns on the right of the table ("Total $ given" and "Max $ given") contain the most important pieces of information in the table. The "Total" column simply shows the total lifetime dollar amount given for the alums at each of the 20 gift capacity levels. The "Max" column shows the maximum amount any one alum has given at each of these levels.

TABLE 8.2 Giving Data for More Than 22,000 Alumni Divided into 20 Groups of Roughly 5% Each by Gift Capacity

GROUP	COUNT	TOTAL $ GIVEN	MAX $ GIVEN
1	1,123	34,062	2,005
2	1,122	84,022	4,290
3	1,123	152,741	5,125
4	1,122	151,635	3,810
5	1,123	209,992	7,500
6	1,123	176,071	12,925
7	1,119	132,106	8,200
8	1,126	192,717	50,000
9	1,122	90,865	9,640
10	1,122	105,096	5,415
11	1,124	151,236	14,563
12	1,122	125,477	5,730
13	1,122	155,151	9,395
14	1,123	235,456	13,700
15	1,122	264,139	42,494
16	1,124	410,154	38,241
17	1,122	303,479	24,184
18	1,123	481,784	24,718
19	1,122	628,010	69,711
20	1,123	2,396,810	224,970

We see a pattern that emerges from this table, but it's a little hard to detect. So go ahead and take a look at Table 8.3 and Figure 8.2. Then we'll offer our thoughts.

When we look at these two tables and this one figure, two conclusions emerge for us:

1. There is *some* relationship between gift capacity and giving, but it's not a strong one.
2. If we can believe the gift capacity ratings, there is a huge amount of untapped potential for giving, especially at the highest capacity levels.

Let's start with the first conclusion, that there is not a strong relationship between capacity and giving. How do we arrive at the conclusion? Let's go back to Table 8.2. Now if we just look at the 5% of alums with the lowest giving capacity (Group 1) and the 5% of alums with the highest giving capacity (Group 20), we see that the total lifetime giving goes from $34,062 to $2,396,810. That's a big difference. The wealthiest alums have given about 70 times as much as the least wealthy alums. Also, the most generous alum in the lowest capacity group has given a lifetime total of $2,005, compared to the most generous alum in the highest capacity group, who has given a lifetime total of $224,970. Again, we see a big difference.

But look at what happens in between these two extremes. Things bounce around a lot. For example, let's compare the giving between capacity level 3 and capacity level 12. The total giving amount for the former group is $152,741; the total giving amount for the former group is $125,477. In other words, alums with a much higher giving capacity have given less than alums with a much lower giving capacity.

Further evidence of this "bouncing around" is apparent when you look at Figure 8.2 (a graphic version of Table 8.3). This chart shows the percentage of alums at each of the 20 giving capacity levels who have given $50 or more lifetime to the school. Notice how these percentages dip in the middle of the capacity range.

So let's go back to our conclusion that there is some relationship between gift capacity and giving, but that it's not a strong relationship. Yes, the overall trend of giving goes up with gift capacity, but we can in no way conclude that knowledge of an alum's gift capacity is a good indication of how much he or she has given.

How about our second conclusion, that there is a huge amount of untapped potential for giving, especially at the highest capacity levels? We think Figure 8.2 provides plenty of support for that conclusion. Look at the highest gift capacity level. Barely 50% of the alums in this category have given more than $50 lifetime. Not as a single gift. No. *Lifetime*.

If that doesn't convince you of the untapped potential for giving among such wealthy alums, we're not sure anything will.

At this point we said you should have someone build you a simple affinity model using some very basic information stored on each alum. That model could take the form of a simple score, such as the four-point score we showed you in the first case

TABLE 8.3   Percentage of Alums Giving $50 or More Lifetime by Gift Capacity Level

GROUP	PERCENT OF ALUMS GIVING $50 OR MORE LIFETIME
1	12.4%
2	23.3%
3	27.5%
4	30.4%
5	34.2%
6	26.9%
7	24.9%
8	26.4%
9	22.1%
10	28.1%
11	29.4%
12	31.6%
13	36.3%
14	38.5%
15	42.3%
16	45.7%
17	41.8%
18	46.7%
19	47.0%
20	51.6%

FIGURE 8.2   Percentage of Alums Giving $50 or More Lifetime by Gift Capacity Level

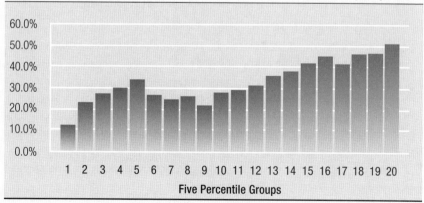

study in chapter 7. Or you could find someone with knowledge of statistics who could create a model using multiple regression. As we've mentioned before, if that person does not already work in your department, you might be able to track down a stats professor in the psychology or education department, a graduate student pursuing a degree in that area, or someone who works in institutional research. Whoever it is, they must be able to explain things in plain English, they must have experience using a statistical software package, and they must have some experience with multiple regression.

That person will build you a simple affinity model using some very basic information stored on each alum for whom you have a capacity rating. For the benefit of that person, we've described below how we developed the model for the school we're using as an example. We've tried to provide just enough detail to give your person a guide. Enclosed in the boxes below (so you can skip over it if you wish) is a summary of what we did.

We chose lifetime hard credit giving as our dependent variable. To each record we added one dollar of giving to arbitrarily rid the sample of zero givers. We then performed a log to the base 10 transformation on this variable to reduce as much of the positive skewness as possible.

We chose the following predictors (independent variables) for entry into our multiple regression analysis:

- MARITAL STATUS MISSING (the alum was given a 1 if there was no marital status listed for him/her in the database, otherwise a 0)

- MARITAL STATUS SINGLE (the alum was given a 1 if he/she was listed as "single" in the database, otherwise a 0)

- CLASS YEAR (the alum's preferred year of graduation)

- THE SQUARE OF THE CLASS YEAR

- HOME PHONE LISTED (a 1 if a home phone was listed in the database for the alum, otherwise a 0)

- BUSINESS PHONE LISTED (a 1 if a business phone was listed in the database for the alum, otherwise a 0)

- EVENT ATTENDED (a 1 if an alum was listed as ever attending an event after graduation, otherwise a 0)

- EMAIL LISTED (a 1 if an email address was listed in the database for the alum, otherwise a 0)

TABLE 8.4   Regression Analysis Table for the Simple Model Developed for This Study

SOURCE	SUM OF SQUARES	df	MEAN SQUARE	F-RATIO
Regression	7213.27	8	901.659	932
Residual	21701.5	22437	0.967218	
VARIABLE	COEFFICIENTS	s.e. OF COEFF	t-RATIO	PROB
Constant	−1603.28	218.2	−7.35	<0.0001
MARITAL STATUS MISSING	−0.333961	0.01845	−18.1	<0.0001
MARITAL STATUS SINGLE	−0.472877	0.01603	−29.5	<0.0001
HP LISTED	0.243367	0.01496	16.3	<0.0001
BP LISTED	0.685641	0.03374	20.3	<0.0001
CLASS YEAR	1.64819	0.2196	7.51	<0.0001
SQUARE OF CLASS YEAR	−4.23E-04	5.52E-05	−7.66	<0.0001
EVENT ATTENDED (YES/NO)	0.712603	0.05089	14	<0.0001
EMAIL LISTED	0.422934	0.01487	28.4	<0.0001

R squared = 24.9%
R squared (adjusted) = 24.9%
S = 0.9835 with 22446 − 9 = 22437 degrees of freedom

Table 8.4 summarizes the results of the regression analysis. We divided the predicted scores from the regression for alums with the highest gift capacity into 20 roughly equal-sized groups where 1 was low and 20 was high.

In the boxed-in technical suggestion, the last thing we say is that we divided the predicted scores from the regression analysis for alums with the highest gift capacity into 20 roughly equal-sized groups, where 1 was low and 20 was high. What does this mean?

Let's start with the specific group of alumni we're most interested in looking at. These are the 1,123 alums who got the highest gift capacity ratings. If you go all the way back to Table 8.1 (which you don't really need to do), you'll see that their total gift capacity is $405,958,000—a lot of money. Our regression analysis created a very granular affinity score for this group. It had 408 different levels. The alums with the lowest of these scores (according to the regression analysis) are least likely to give a lot of money to the school; the alums with the highest of these scores are the most likely to give a lot of money to the school.

That's terrific, but 408 score levels are too many levels to make any practical use of. So we took those scores and chopped them up into 20 roughly equal sized groups from 1 to 20, where (again) 1 represents the lowest scores and 20 represents the highest scores. Detailed giving data on all these 1,123 alums is displayed in Table 8.5 below.

TABLE 8.5 Giving Data for More Than 1,123 Very High Gift Capacity Alumni Divided into 20 Groups of Roughly 5% Each by Affinity Score

GROUP	COUNT	SUM	MEAN	MEDIAN	MAX
1	56	$430	$8	–	$85
2	56	$1,320	$24	–	$385
3	56	$570	$10	–	$135
4	53	$17,870	$337	–	$11,000
5	59	$9,439	$160	$10	$2,465
6	52	$8,605	$165	$20	$2,510
7	59	$13,396	$227	$15	$4,705
8	48	$11,220	$234	$23	$3,265
9	64	$52,970	$828	$20	$28,761
10	45	$26,594	$591	$100	$10,650
11	57	$138,290	$2,426	$115	$103,110
12	67	$22,880	$341	$65	$4,110
13	42	$94,985	$2,262	$25	$78,055
14	69	$50,107	$726	$150	$17,204
15	58	$155,018	$2,673	$205	$114,039
16	53	$56,186	$1,060	$190	$17,750
17	55	$269,010	$4,891	$450	$208,995
18	58	$254,315	$4,385	$275	$206,330
19	58	$729,090	$12,571	$1,055	$224,970
20	56	$483,749	$8,638	$1,758	$108,950

Let's move on to our next step: Pick a small group of alums who have a high capacity rating and a high affinity rating. Table 8.5 gives us a lot of information about where we're likely to find this small group. Let's see what looks interesting here. Remember, everyone in this total group of 1,123 alums has a gift capacity rating greater than $116,000. This is a wealthy bunch of folks.

We'll start with the lowest group, Group 1. These 56 alums have the lowest affinity scores of the total group, and their giving data confirms that. Look at the value for these alums in the "sum" column: $430. That means that all 56 alums, as a group, have given less than $500 lifetime to the school. That works out to a mean lifetime gift of less than $8 per alum. Our conclusion? These folks may be wealthy, but both their affinity score and their history of giving have them speaking loud and clear: "Our philanthropic interests are aimed at worthy causes other than our alma mater."

Now let's jump up to the top group, Group 20. Notice that there are exactly the same number of alumni in this group as in Group 1 (56), but the giving data for this top group is quite different from that of the bottom group. Most notably, they've given a total of $483,789, well over a thousand times as much as the bottom group. So here we have a group of alums who (a) we know are wealthy, (b) have a high affinity rating developed from the regression analysis, and (c) have already given the school quite a bit of money.

The final step is to study the alumni in this small group and identify some who may deserve more scrutiny. It's time to take a very close look at this group in Table 8.6 below. It lists the total giving and gift capacity for each of these 56 records. Remember, each of the 56 alums has a high gift capacity rating, and each has an affinity score that says they really like the school.

We'll start off with a couple of alums who have already given a considerable amount to the school. What's particularly interesting about these two is how different they look from the perspective of the possibility of very large future gifts.

- Record #1: From the looks of things, this person is probably well-known to the research staff and to the gift officers. The person has given more than $100,000 and has a gift capacity that's not a whole lot more than that amount. We're pretty sure the school would like to have a lot more alums like this one.

- Record #7: We find this one pretty interesting. The alum has given a bit over $21,000 lifetime, but this person's gift capacity is listed as well over $13 million. Since the alum clearly likes the school, and he (or she) has considerable wherewithal to give a lot more, why hasn't this alum done so? Maybe there's a good reason, maybe not. At the very least, this is someone who deserves continued attention both from the prospect research side of the house and the gift officer side of the house.

Now we'll move down to five alums (Records #15, 17, 18, 20, and 24), all of whom have given less than $6,000 lifetime but whose gift capacity ratings all exceed $400,000. Here we are probably in the neighborhood of prospects who truly are flying under the radar. They may have been assigned to a gift officer. And when a prospect researcher looks at their profiles, the researcher may say, "Yeah, we know about him." But our experience tells us that alums like these are worth a harder look. For example, we would ask:

- Is the alum really assigned to a gift officer, or did the last gift officer simply write the alum off as not a "good prospect" with no good documentation as to why that decision was made?

- What does the alum do for a living? Does that occupation (e.g., investment banker) jibe with the gift capacity rating?

- Has the alum been an active volunteer or event attendee?

- Is he or she at the age where a sizeable planned gift might be a possibility?

TABLE 8.6   Giving and Gift Capacity Data for All 56 Alums in the Highest Affinity Group

RECORD	TOTAL GIFTS	GIFT CAPACITY	RECORD	TOTAL GIFTS	GIFT CAPACITY
1	$108,950	$151,965	29	$1,685	$135,375
2	$59,235	$643,823	30	$1,675	$206,030
3	$58,498	$667,752	31	$1,600	$359,840
4	$37,700	$455,684	32	$1,390	$221,603
5	$36,660	$1,478,588	33	$1,325	$323,879
6	$30,850	$738,029	34	$1,260	$147,358
7	$21,150	$13,334,283	35	$1,230	$501,206
8	$13,639	$273,923	36	$1,050	$124,368
9	$8,075	$137,125	37	$1,025	$142,682
10	$7,915	$144,669	38	$975	$132,261
11	$7,683	$155,998	39	$800	$215,234
12	$7,175	$131,594	40	$799	$343,891
13	$6,920	$227,085	41	$780	$448,043
14	$6,525	$148,666	42	$765	$152,909
15	$5,850	$484,761	43	$605	$960,662
16	$5,810	$211,779	44	$600	$125,605
17	$5,365	$636,545	45	$505	$125,502
18	$4,400	$557,772	46	$500	$118,003
19	$4,085	$291,005	47	$475	$193,034
20	$3,915	$473,962	48	$425	$133,835
21	$3,765	$148,890	49	$400	$542,528
22	$3,690	$187,921	50	$400	$260,654
23	$3,490	$134,685	51	$325	$300,091
24	$2,660	$474,012	52	$250	$177,278
25	$2,485	$274,909	53	$50	$221,333
26	$2,430	$4,367,348	54	$50	$120,614
27	$2,055	$267,489	55	–	$260,442
28	$1,830	$631,781	56	–	$25,798,989

You get the idea. With folks like these we think you should dig a little. Some of them may be at what Malcolm Gladwell calls "the tipping point." They may be right on the verge of making a much larger gift if you do a little more research on them and send the right gift officer out to meet with them.

By the way, take a look at Record #56. This person is really rich, and the internal data says he or she really likes the school, but this person hasn't given any money. We'd sure like to know the story about this person.

Considerations for Prospect Research

What if your school has done some data mining but has not invested in a wealth screening? Now you've got an affinity-related score, but you have no way to narrow the list down based on capacity. The task of using a set of scores to determine propensity to make a major gift falls to someone working in prospect research. The risk is that the prospect researcher will be asked to produce in-depth profiles of the top 100 or 200 unfamiliar names by score … an impossible task.

If there is no way around having to do old-fashioned research, then limit research to "top level" information only: job title and company, giving history with the institution, maybe their Who's Who profile if it exists—and not much more. A better, more focused approach is to take the top several hundred prospects (according to propensity score) and sort them in descending order by lifetime giving. Think of the propensity score as summing up the affinity that the prospect feels for the institution. The lifetime giving dollar amount provides evidence not only of affinity but of capacity as well. If a prospect has a very high affinity score and has given in five figures, she's probably a good major-gift prospect. Take the top 10 or so unfamiliar names and do in-depth profiles on them alone, leaving the others for later.

If fundraisers are insisting on in-depth profiles for each and every prospect they've never met, there might be larger issues, ones more difficult to deal with directly: They don't understand the process for prospect identification, they lack confidence in its ability to deliver good prospects, and they don't have a plan for approaching people they know little or nothing about. Those are problems that can only be addressed by communication, a certain amount of selling on the part of the data miner, and a lot of support from upper management.

Another issue: Prospect researchers know that wealth screening data becomes outdated, but what about modeling scores? Constituent giving and age change over time, but does that matter? Maybe it depends on what model you use and the variables that go into it?

The general answer is yes, scores from a predictive model do get "stale," although they may not become merely outdated in the same way that wealth screening data does. They may become less relevant over time. Or, rather, they may not be as effective as they might be, lacking the benefit of recent data. Given the volume of interactions and transactions that might occur over a year (gifts, events attended, surveys responded to, etc.), it's probably a good idea to have fresh scores every year. Changes in the age of constituents is not as much a factor, because all constituents age at the same rate—which is not true of changes in behaviors such as giving.

Institutions with in-house capability are at an advantage because they can build models continuously—each iteration of the model will lead to improvements (one hopes)—at an attractive cost per model. As the saying goes, every model is wrong, but some are useful. Re-scoring constituents is as much about getting it "less wrong" as it is about being up to date.

For Kevin, summertime has always been model-building season. The latest graduates have been loaded into the alumni database, the scores will be needed for annual giving appeals in September, and it's worked out that summers have been less hectic than other times of year. In general, though, for institutions with in-house capability, there is only one sure time to create a new model: Whenever there's a business problem that requires one.

chapter 9

Planned Giving
Increasing the Chances of Success

O f any type of fundraising involving prospect identification, perhaps none is as challenging as planned giving. And yet, in no other area (aside from major giving) can some smart prospecting yield such a significant return.

The term *planned gift* encompasses a variety of giving vehicles, the most familiar being the bequest: leaving something in one's will. The planned gift allows even a donor of modest means to make a gift comparable in size to a major gift. The fact that such a gift often springs not from wealth but from a high degree of affinity with your organization or cause means that many of these donors fly under the radar of our traditional prospect identification tools. A wealth screening, for example, will fail to identify many of your best prospects.

For this reason, many institutions are not as good at prospect identification for planned giving as they ought to be. A program might be growing, but the source of the growth will be donors who self-identify by approaching fundraising staff for information or who become known to the institution once they have died and their estate is about to be distributed according to their wishes. In either case, there is little or no opportunity for planned giving professionals to discuss estate planning options. Not to mention that it's hard to make any forecasts when most of one's gifts are coming in "over the transom." There's a level of unpredictability that one does not see in, say, annual giving.

Imagine, though, if planned giving officers were able to identify good prospects earlier on. Imagine if the average age of your expectancies were lower than it is now, with more opportunities to build the relationship and achieve the mix of vehicle, designation, and recognition that is right for both donor and institution. That would be worth something, wouldn't it?

Modeling for predicting propensity to engage in planned giving is trickier than other types of modeling because, compared with annual giving, there's just not as much data to work with. Predictive modeling requires a certain amount of historical data in which to sift for characteristics associated with the desired behavior we're trying to model. If you already have many donors of a certain type, you're better able to identify the characteristics that flag similar individuals in the non-donor pool. No past donor data, no model.

For planned giving, your existing pool of expectancies is probably small, both in absolute terms and as a proportion of your total alumni population. The haystack is huge and the needles are few. Experts will offer you advice on the traits that characterize good prospects for planned giving ("many small gifts over time" is a common assumption), but when you approach the problem from a predictive modeling point of view, your job is to study many traits (i.e., variables) in your own data—and *not* to rely on assumptions or rules of thumb. The approach is, not to reject rules of thumb, but to test them. In other words, try to convert the assumptions into useable facts, if the data supports doing so.

Fortunately, for this type of model we are free to use variables based on past giving behavior, which is something we can't do with a propensity-to-give model. Why? Because our predicted value in such a model is "Giving"—and we can't use Giving to predict giving. But for our planned giving model, our predicted value is a binary Yes/No value (1 for Yes, 0 for No), with Yes meaning the individual is a planned giving expectancy, No for everyone else. That's not the same as "Giving."

One example of a variable based on giving is a simple total of the number of years in which a constituent has made a gift. According to expert opinion in the field of planned giving, an institution's best prospects are those with the greatest number of years of giving, regardless of the size of gift. There's some database query work involved here, but if you can count up the number of years that an individual has given a gift, for all the years you have data, you've got a good variable to work with. Let's say your institution has 20 years of donor data, so your values for this variable will range from 0 to 20.

In the case study that follows, we'll score some real data based on years of giving, and then show you the advantages of going well beyond just that.

A slightly more complicated giving-history variable is "Frequency," calculated using this formula:

$$\text{Frequency} = \frac{\text{Number of gifts}}{(\text{Last year of giving} - \text{First year of giving} + 1)}$$

In other words, "Frequency" is equal to the number of lifetime gifts made by the donor, divided by the number of years the individual has been a donor. If a donor has given only once, the result will be 1. All non-donors have a frequency of zero. Why plus one in the denominator? Unless you add a year, the calculation of the number of years an individual has been a donor will always be off by one year. For example, if a donor gave once per year in 2005, 2006, 2007, 2008, and 2009 (five gifts, five years, so once per year) then the formula would give $5 / (2009 - 2005) = 5/4 = 1.25$ gifts per year, which is inaccurate. The +1 in the denominator will turn this into $5 / (2009 - 2005 + 1) = 5/(4+1) = 5/5 = 1$, which is the correct one gift per year. In the case of a single year of giving, it prevents the dividing-by-zero error.

Again, there's some work involved: You'll need to query the database for the minimum and maximum fiscal years of everyone's giving records, and then you'll need to create some derived variables in your stats or modeling software to create the variable. You'll also need to decide whether to count monthly gifts as 12 gifts per year or as a single gift. The variable that results will have non-zero values that can range from a small fraction of a gift per year up to any number of gifts per year. Keep in mind that if a donor has a Frequency of 0.1, that doesn't describe actual giving behavior (i.e., making one-tenth of a gift per year), but only means her giving is probably quite sparse and thinly spread over time in comparison to other donors.

LOOKING BEYOND DONOR LOYALTY

We identified current planned giving expectancies in one school's alumni database, and pulled giving totals for the 20 fiscal years prior to their identification. To select the group, we chose everyone identified as an expectancy in the year 2003 or later, so the years of giving were 1983 to 2002. We also limited the group to people who are now at least 50 years old. This ensured that everyone in the group was probably old enough to have participated in the annual fund during any of those years, if they chose.

We didn't look at how much they gave, only *whether* they gave in a given year. Expectancies who gave in 20 out of 20 years received a score of 20. Someone who had given in 10 years out of 20 got a score of 10, and so on. Non-donors were scored as zero.

Then we made a bar chart of their scores, seen in Figure 9.1. The height of the bars shows the percentage of the group that falls into each number of years of giving in that 20-year span.

What does Figure 9.1 tell us? It's clear these expectancies are indeed very loyal donors. A little under half of them have some giving in at least 10 of the 20 years. That's wonderful. Notice that quite a lot of current expectancies have no giving in any of the past 20 years. There might be something to explain this. Maybe the current expectancy record is actually the spouse of an alum. It would not be a rare thing for a surviving widow to have no giving, even if she is an alum, since at some institutions the male spouse in a two-alum household is often given hard credit for gifts. At any rate, that's not what we are primarily interested in.

FIGURE 9.1 Percent Planned Giving Alums by Years of Giving

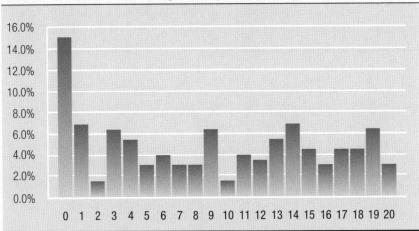

In order to really understand what this means, we need something to compare against. Figure 9.2 shows the same chart, but with all alumni over 50 who are *not* current expectancies.

Big difference! Because of the disproportionate number of non-donors in this group, the scale is totally different. As a percentage of alumni, very loyal donors are scarce. Let's look at it another way, excluding non-donors from both groups. In Figure 9.3, the expectancy donors have giving in twice as many years as non-expectancy donors, on average.

No wonder, then, we've been told to focus on loyal annual fund donors in order to identify new prospects for planned giving. The connection is undeniable.

A couple of things interfere with the clarity of this picture, however. Have another look at Figure 9.1. There's really no definite pattern to it, is there. Although planned giving expectancies have been good annual fund donors, they are all over the map in terms of loyalty. All of these people are old enough to have contributed in every

FIGURE 9.2 Percent Non-Planned Giving Alums by Years of Giving

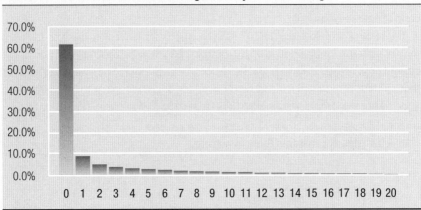

FIGURE 9.3 Mean Years with Giving, 1983–2002

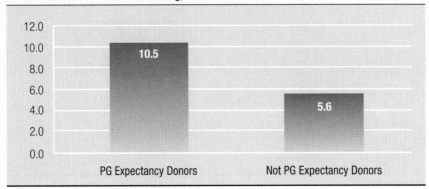

year since 1983, but a significant percentage of them have given in only a handful of years. For example, 6% of current expectancies have giving in only ONE of the 20 years. They share that distinction with 10,000 alumni who are *not* expectancies.

In other words, if years of giving was your only metric for proactively identifying prospects, and no expectancies came in "over the transom," that 6% of the group would never be discovered. There are just too many individuals at the lower end of years-of-giving to get focused in any practical way. Donor loyalty is therefore a great predictor of planned giving potential, but it is far from definitive.

If giving history provides only a partial answer, where else should you look? We have a few ideas.

Using the same group of current expectancies (age 50 or older, and identified in 2003 or later), we pulled some other characteristics from the database to test as predictors. We were careful to select data that existed before 2003, i.e., that pre-dated the identification of the individuals as expectancies.

Here's a great one: student activities. Participation in varsity sports, campus clubs, and student government is coded in the database, and Figure 9.4 compares the proportions of the people in the two groups who have at least one such activity code in their records.

Interesting, eh? Now, maybe 10 or 15 years ago there was a big push on to solicit former athletes for planned giving, and that's why they're well represented in the current crop of expectancies—but we doubt that very much. The evidence indicates that student experience is a big factor even for decisions taken many years later. This is a great example of how even the oldest data is valuable in the present day.

FIGURE 9.4 Has at Least One Student Activity

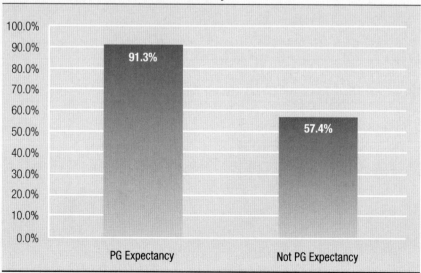

FIGURE 9.5 Holds More Than One Degree

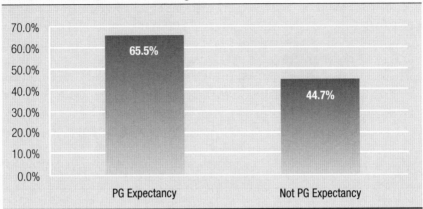

Here's another one: alumni who hold more than one degree. The proportions on both sides are high, because we counted degrees from *any* university (that information happens to be available in the database), and this university has many graduate and professional degree holders. Figure 9.5 would seem to indicate that expectancies are more likely to hold multiple degrees than are non-expectancies. A little more digging would tell us whether a particular profession (doctors or lawyers, for example) are heavily represented among the expectancies group, or whether earning more than one degree from the same university is more important than just having multiple degrees.

In our data, we also created a variable for the presence of a Faculty or Staff code, which indicates whether someone is or at one time was employed by the university. This code is not uniformly applied (it does not directly correspond to actual employment data), so it's not perfect, but as a rough indicator it works fine for data mining. See Figure 9.6.

FIGURE 9.6 Faculty or Staff Code Present

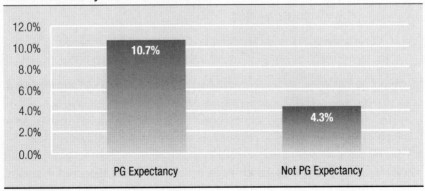

FIGURE 9.7   Has Attended at Least One Event

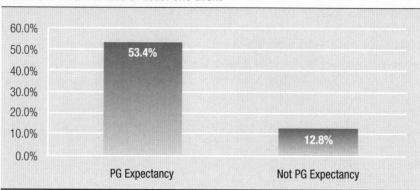

Next up is one of Kevin's favorite predictors for planned giving potential: event attendance. We've seen this elsewhere, and it holds true here as well. Showing up at any kind of reunion or alumni-related event is highly predictive. We've excluded attendance at any kind of donor-recognition event—if only donors are invited, attendance is mostly a proxy for "is a donor." See Figure 9.7.

We could do this for a dozen more variables, but you get the point: Your current expectancies have characteristics that set them apart from most other donors, and you can use these differences as predictors of planned giving potential. Note, of course, that *our* predictors are not necessarily *your* predictors. It's up to you to do a little digging and find them.

From here, we could nitpick about whether some of these predictors are really better than "donor loyalty," but by this point you should know that you don't have to choose just one characteristic and run with it—you can combine a number of characteristics into a powerful score. Devise a simple scoring system that gives one point for "donor loyalty" (however you wish to define that—we've defined it as giving in at least 10 years out of 20) and one point for each of the other predictors that strike you as particularly powerful. Using the predictors we've presented here, our score would be calculated like so:

Loyal donor (0/1) + Student activity (0/1) + Multiple degrees (0/1)
+ Faculty or Staff (0/1) + Event attendance (0/1) = Maximum PG score of 5

What happens when we apply this model to score the database? Out of more than 30,000 living and addressable alumni over the age of 50 who are not already expectancies, only 89 have a perfect score of 5 out of 5. That's a very manageable, high-quality list of individuals to provide for review by a planned giving officer.

This model is far from the last word in data mining for planned giving, and it has some severe limitations. For example, focusing on these 89 individuals might essentially result in a campaign based solely on retired professors in your School of Medicine! Your expectancies are not going to be one homogeneous group, so you'll want to identify other clusters for solicitation. As well, when we drop the bar to include alumni with a score of 4 out of 5, almost 700 individuals pop out of this database, so things get out of hand quickly when you have too few score levels.

Otherwise, it's pretty nifty. This score is easy to understand, not terribly difficult to calculate, and is a useful departure from any single-minded focus on donor loyalty.

Even more so than in other areas of fundraising, planned giving officers and data miners need to work together so that everyone understands what's being delivered by the model: a segment of the population that is most likely to contain PG-positive people, *not* a list of sure winners. Predictive modeling is just the first step; development officers know they must still qualify prospects and that cultivation can take a long time before a gift emerges.

Final Thoughts on Modeling for Planned Giving

We hope you'll pay some attention to our suggestion that external data or old, worn-out assumptions won't be nearly as useful for identifying new prospects as a predictive model based on a few well-chosen, affinity-related variables from your internal data. Planned giving does, however, present a few special challenges for modeling.

Naturally, the number of constituents in your database who are already engaged in the behavior of interest—that is, who are known expectancies—will be small in relation to the total size of the population. Having fewer examples of the type of person you're looking for will make it harder to generalize about what characteristics you should be paying attention to.

A specific example: Kevin once built a model for planned giving for a university that had a long history of being a Catholic institution but had since developed a more secular character. Still, though, retired priests formed a community living on campus. When they died, they often left their estates to the university. In Kevin's model, therefore, it was not surprising that having "Rev." as a name prefix emerged as a significant predictor of planned giving potential. Unfortunately, what was true of the past was not necessarily still true. It simply was not the case that the university's future expectancies would come from the ranks of retired clergy. The model fit the current data very well—too well, in fact. Would it be relevant for prospect identification in the future? Not very likely, given how the university culture had changed.

In predictive modeling, there is a technical term for this sort of nontechnical example. It's called *overfitting.* That's when a model is an excellent fit with historical data but does a poor job with new data. It can be a problem when examples of your target variable are sparse—common with planned giving.

Some analysts will include deceased donors in their models in order to increase the numbers of individuals on which to model on. There will be valid data there, but over time these records which have ceased to change will become out of date and may fail to adequately describe the type of person who will consider planned giving in the future. If you do include records of deceased individuals, don't go too far back in time. People who have been deceased for no longer than five years is a limit we have seen used effectively.

Boosting the size of the "target" is one way to proceed; another is to reduce the total size of the haystack that you have to search through. If it seems highly unlikely that anyone under the age of 40 or 45 is going to be approached about planned giving, then eliminate them from your data. Focusing on the true population of interest is a key starting point in building models that work.

chapter 10

The Last Word

From the outset, we knew we wanted to speak to two sides of the advancement organization: the decision-makers judging the value of investing in in-house analytical capacity, and the employees who would actually do the work and unleash the power residing in data.

We've done the best we can. Before we sign off, though, a few closing thoughts.

To the decision-makers we say, university advancement offices are in an advantageous position compared with businesses and organizations in the private sector, believe it or not. When businesses weigh an investment in analytics they're often counting the cost of a whole lot of stuff that you don't have to. Think of database software, data warehouses, querying and reporting software, server hardware, and IT support, plus investments in data governance, security, and just the gathering of the data itself. Universities and many nonprofit organizations have made these investments already. Investing in analytics is more like harvesting the fruit of all that has been sown over the years. If you fail to analyze your own data, you forego returns on what are essentially sunk costs.

To the employees we say, data analysis is a rewarding, challenging, and above all *fun* line of work that will provide much value to your employer and a stepping-stone in career advancement to you. There is no downside to doing whatever it takes to acquire skills in this area. Keep playing, exploring and asking questions of your data. Visit the CoolData blog (*cooldata.org*) and subscribe to receive email alerts when new posts are added. As long as we're able, we'll continue to post about topics in predictive analytics and data analysis as they relate to advancement for educational institutions and nonprofits, including case studies like the ones in this book.

To all of you have taken the time to read some or all of this book:
Thanks.

Nonfiction books are not like novels. With novels we usually read them all the way through to the end (unless they're awful). We want to find out what happens. Not so with nonfiction books; there's no suspenseful ending to keep us plowing through them. So it's the rare one who reads a nonfiction book in its entirety. Neither of us can remember the last one we read all the way through. So ... If you've read even a small portion of this thing, thanks. If you've read through the whole darn thing, thanks a bunch!

Put the book down for a couple of weeks and then go through it again.
We know. Seems inconsistent with what we just said about our own reading habits. But here's what Peter does: He almost always underlines any nonfiction book he reads. If it's a book he really likes, he'll go back to it many times and read only what he's underlined. Invariably, something has happened between now and the last reading that causes him to appreciate what he's underlined in more depth. Some of these books are decades old and are held together with tape or staples. "Be delighted if that's the way your copy of this book looks long after I'm gone," he says. (Guess you don't need tape or staples for e-books though.)

Lend the book to a colleague whose judgment and opinions you respect.
It's always good to get another point of view from someone who has a good head on her shoulders. She can point out stuff you missed when you read the book. She can challenge ideas we've offered that you've just accepted because were "experts." And most of all, if she knows you well, she can suggest steps you can take that you might be reluctant to take. Like showing some more backbone with a problem boss or a challenging employee.

Within your own office: If you're the boss, hand the book down to someone who you think can make something happen with it. If you're on staff, hand it up to someone you think might "get it."

Find another book that touches on the same topics as this one but offers some different ideas.
We might feel a little threatened if you end up liking that book better than you do ours. We'll get over it.

If you like the book, let other people know about it.
CASE and we two are going to promote the heck out of this book. But the best promotion will come from folks like you. Even if you don't like the book and are vocal

about it with your friends and colleagues. Any publicity, good or bad, is ultimately good publicity … not because it sells books, but because it keeps people focused on something we both care deeply about.

Thanks again,
Peter Wylie @pbradwylie
Kevin MacDonell @kevinmacdonell

Index

Figures, notes, and tables are indicated by *italic f, n,* and *t,* respectively.

About CASE

The **Council for Advancement and Support of Education** (CASE) is a professional association serving educational institutions and the advancement professionals who work on their behalf in alumni relations, communications, development, marketing, and allied areas. Founded in 1974, CASE maintains headquarters in Washington, D.C., with offices in London, Singapore, and Mexico City. Its membership includes more than 3,500 colleges and universities, primary and secondary independent and international schools, and nonprofit organizations in 76 countries. CASE serves more than 70,000 advancement professionals on the staffs of its member institutions and has more than 17,000 professional members on its roster. CASE also offers a variety of advancement products and services, provides standards and an ethical framework for the profession, and works with other organizations to respond to public issues of concern while promoting the importance of education worldwide.